The Routledge Atlas of Central Eurasian Affairs

Providing concisely written entries on the most important current issues in Central Asia and Eurasia, this atlas offers relevant background information on the region's place in the contemporary political and economic world.

Features include:

- Profiles of the constituent countries of Central Asia, namely Kazakhstan, Kyrgyzstan, Tajikistan, Turkmenistan and Uzbekistan
- Profiles of Mongolia, western China, Tibet, and the three Caucasus states of Armenia, Azerbaijan and Georgia
- Timely and significant original maps and data for each entry
- A comprehensive glossary, places index and subject index of major concepts, terms and regional issues
- A bibliography and a useful websites section

Designed for use in teaching undergraduate and graduate classes and seminars in geography, history, economics, anthropology, international relations, political science and the environment, as well as regional courses on the former Soviet Union, Central Asia, and Eurasia, this atlas is also a comprehensive reference source for libraries and scholars interested in these fields.

Stanley D. Brunn is Professor of Geography at the University of Kentucky, USA. He has published widely on world cities, US cities, political, social and economic geography, the geographies of communication and cyberspace, peace, images and identities, Wal-Mart and the geographies of 9/11. He has had extensive travel, teaching and research experience in Kazakhstan, Kyrgyzstan and Tajikistan over the past several decades.

Stanley W. Toops is an Associate Professor of Geography and International Studies at Miami University, USA. His research in geography and international studies has focused on the Central Asian portion of China, the Xinjiang Uyghur Autonomous Region. He has had extensive travel and research experience in China (particularly Xinjiang and Tibet), Mongolia, Kazakhstan, Kyrgyzstan, Uzbekistan and Pakistan since 1985.

Richard Gilbreath is Director of the Gyula Pauer Center for Cartography and GIS at the University of Kentucky, USA.

The Routledge Atlas of Central Eurasian Affairs

Stanley D. Brunn, Stanley W. Toops and Richard Gilbreath

Routledge
Taylor & Francis Group

LONDON AND NEW YORK

First published 2012
by Routledge
2 Park Square, Milton Park, Abingdon, Oxon OX14 4RN

Simultaneously published in the USA and Canada
by Routledge
711 Third Avenue, New York, NY 10017

Routledge is an imprint of the Taylor & Francis Group, an informa business

British Library Cataloguing in Publication Data
A catalogue record for this book is available from the British Library

Library of Congress Cataloging in Publication Data
Brunn, Stanley D.
  The Routledge atlas of Central Eurasian affairs/Stanley D. Brunn,
  Stanley W. Toops, and Richard Gilbreath.
  p. cm.
  Includes bibliographical references and indexes.
  1. Asia, Central – Historical geography – Maps. 2. Asia, Central –
  Politics and government – Maps. 3. Asia, Central – Economic
  conditions – Maps. 4. Eurasia – Historical geography – Maps.
  5. Eurasia – Politics and government – Maps. 6. Eurasia –
  Economic conditions – Maps. I. Toops, Stanley.
  II. Gilbreath, Richard. III. Title. IV. Title: Atlas of
  Central Eurasian affairs.
  G2166.S1B7 2012
  911'.58 – dc23   2011046941

ISBN: 978-0-415-49750-3 (hbk)
ISBN: 978-0-415-49752-7 (pbk)
ISBN: 978-0-203-11856-6 (ebk)

Typeset in Times New Roman
by Florence Production Ltd, Stoodleigh, Devon

Printed and bound in Great Britain by the MPG Books Group

Contents

Preface

The first two editors, with major interests in the former Soviet Union and especially Central Asia, discussed in mid-2010 the idea of an atlas of the region. Interest in the project stemmed from the lack of an inexpensive, comprehensive and region-wide atlas that could and would be useful to career professionals in government, NGOs and the business world and also to professionals in the social sciences and humanities in North America, Europe, Asia and especially in Central Asia.

Once we agreed on the idea for such a reference source, the next question was what would be the geographical extent (north–south and east–west)? While there was no question that the five former Soviet republics in Central Asia would be included as they are now independent states on the world political map, discussion mostly centered on whether to include the Caucasus states, Mongolia and even China's western provinces. After serious deliberation, we agreed the atlas would include all of the above and we would refer to this region as Central Eurasia, a most fitting label for this section of the huge Eurasian continent.

As Routledge, a major international publisher with a reputation for publishing timely regional and country books on a wide variety of economic, environmental, social and political topics, had already published an *Atlas of World Affairs* by Andrew Boyd and Joshua Comenetz in 2007, we decided to approach the company. We were very pleased with the initial positive reaction to our prospectus. They issued us a contract and were in agreement with the content we proposed and that the cartography should be completed by Richard Gilbreath, the third editor, who is Director of the Gyula Pauer Center for Cartography and GIS at the University of Kentucky. Dick is a very accomplished and professional cartographer; that he has previously served as a cartographer on other atlases, of Southeast Asia and Kentucky, attests to the high quality of his efforts. Because of his major role in this atlas project, we decided to include him in the author team, a decision that was easy to make.

While Dick conducted research for and prepared most of the maps, he also had assistance from undergraduate geography majors, Brit Frasure, Matthew Basanta, Stephanie Shaw and Ted Smith. They learned from him not only the joy that comes from constructing high-quality and useful maps, but also the importance of meeting deadlines, checking data sources and critiquing finished products. Others whom we thank for their important support for the project are Ken Grabach, Miami University Libraries; William Renwick, Chair, Department of Geography, Miami University; and Sue Roberts, Chair, Department of Geography, University of Kentucky. Stanley Toops also thanks Professors Kuei-sheng Chang, W. A. Douglas Jackson and Ilse Cirtautas, his professors at the University of Washington, where he was first introduced to Central Eurasia. Simone Andrus provided much needed support for this project. Stanley Brunn would like to thank Natalya Tyutenkova for sharing valuable insights and experiences on contemporary and historical Central Eurasia, and also Alan de Young and Galina Valyayeva for sharing their vast experiences in Central Eurasian culture and education in the past decade. Finally, our thanks to Dorothea Schaefter, Editor for Asian Studies, Jillian Morrison, Senior Editorial Assistant for Asian Studies, Lisa Salonen, Senior Production Editor, and Carol Fellingham-Web for her copy-editing; in fact, we are most grateful to the entire Routledge team for their support in shepherding us in the initial stages and throughout the production process.

Stanley D. Brunn
Stanley W. Toops
Richard A. Gilbreath
Lexington, Kentucky

1   Introduction

The label and definition of Eurasia has long been used by a wide variety of scholars in the humanities and social sciences. It is generally defined as the expanse of territory that extends from western Russia eastward to the Pacific Ocean and south to include most of China and what is today considered Central Asia and also the Caucasus. Excluded from this broad definition are the Indian subcontinent, Iran and countries in southwest Asia. While there is general agreement on the Eurasian label and territorial definition, there is much less agreement on what is considered Central Eurasia, the regional definition used for this atlas. During the time of the Soviet Union, that label would and could easily have been used to define the five Central Asian Soviet republics or "stans." In a post-Soviet world, the territorial extent of what is considered Central Eurasia is somewhat a matter of individual scholarly tastes and also sensitivity to using a Soviet territorial label, namely Central Asia. The controversy extends to discussions among scholars about exactly how far "west" a region called Central Eurasia would reach, and also how far "east," especially with the awakening of China in the global marketplace, global entrepreneurial space and global geopolitical dialogues. Questions about the eastern extent need to weigh which, if any, provinces of western China might legitimately be included in Central Eurasia and also whether Mongolia should. Questions also arise about the western extent of a Central Eurasian region. The inclusion of Georgia, Azerbaijan and Armenia within Europe has posed a dilemma to more than one European geographer and historian; the same dilemmas arise for the Asian scholar.

We are acutely aware of the controversies among geographers, historians, cultural anthropologists, regional economists and Soviet and post-Soviet political scientists regarding decisions as to whether Caucasus states, Mongolia or China's western provinces legitimately merit inclusion in a Central Eurasian region. While we recognize the merits, the geography community is probably more concerned about territorial boundaries than are other scholars. That is because we seek to identify those cultural, economic, historical and environmental features that have some overriding similarities or homogeneity. More than one introductory world regional geography textbook or regional text on Europe or the Soviet Union, or now Russia, has discussed the perplexities and difficulties that arise in defining Eurasia or even Central Asia. A perusal of maps in the aforementioned books would attest to the different regional boundaries, especially the western and eastern extents.

Our decision was to include a broad expanse of states and territorial units that best define Central Eurasia. In our initial discussions we had no difficulty agreeing that the five Central Asian former Soviet republics, Kazakhstan, Kyrgyzia (now Kyrgyzstan), Tajikistan, Turkmenia (now Turkmenistan) and Uzbekistan, would be included in Central Asia. There was also little disagreement that Mongolia merited inclusion. There was some discussion regarding Armenia, Azerbaijan and Georgia, as their cultural, historical and environmental geographies were different from those of the Central Asian "stans." However, on balance, it was agreed that they should be included in any Central Eurasian region. Questions also arose about China's three western provinces, Xinjiang, Tibet and Qinghai. Again, on balance, these three administrative units share much more in common culturally with Mongolia, Kazakhstan and Kyrgyzstan than with Han Chinese regions farther east. Thus, they were included.

What is apparent to scholarly communities studying Central Eurasia is that this region has blossomed into a major arena of disciplinary, interdisciplinary and transdisciplinary scholarship since the end of the Soviet Union in 1991. The number of books, chapters and journal articles on this region has truly skyrocketed with contributions both by scholars residing in Central Eurasia today, and especially by those from outside the region. Here we are referring to the listservs on Central Asia, such as CentAsia Listserv, but also websites about countries, university degree programs and conferences, and opportunities for language training, fieldwork and research collaboration. The number of scholars with homes in European, Asian and North American universities is significant. These include not only young scholars focusing their careers on one or more research topics or themes, such as religion, politics or gender issues, but also senior scholars who developed a research interest in Central Eurasia following the end of the Cold War and the increase in opportunities for Central Asian language training, interdisciplinary teaching and fieldwork, and conference organizing and presentations. The intellectual and scholarly renaissance of the past twenty years certainly, in our minds, is significant for what has been accomplished. (This topic in itself would be a most interesting and rewarding thesis or dissertation topic, namely who contributed what and when.)

The plethora of research materials published in the past couple of decades is significant, not only in the volume of what has been produced, but in the variety and quality as well. There are now regular sessions at disciplinary and transdisciplinary national and international conferences on historical and current events, developments and processes in Central Eurasia or subregions, such as the Caucasus or Central Asia, or about individual cities, industrial and tourist regions. Added to this mix of scholarly materials we note, in particular, Bregel's *An Historical Atlas of Central Asia*. Also a number of atlases have appeared which are devoted to specific periods or specific regions. These include Abazov's *The Palgrave Concise Historical Atlas of Central Asia*, and the recent Asian Development Bank's *Central Asia Atlas of Natural Resources*. Many atlases of Russia also cover the Central Asian states including Brawer's *Atlas of Russia and the Independent Republics*, Gilbert's *The Routledge Atlas of Russian History* and Milner-Gulland's *Cultural Atlas of Russia and the Former Soviet Union*. Atlases about China fill in the picture for western China including National Geographic's *Atlas of China*, Benewick and Donald's *The State of China Atlas*, and Chinese Academy of Sciences' *The Atlas of Population, Environment and Sustainable Development of China*.

While on reflection there are a number of atlases that will aid the regional specialists and regional generalists, no standard comprehensive atlas of Central Eurasia exists that would aid both the highly specialized professional and the new aspiring scholarly communities. In short, the materials about historical, economic, social, political, cultural and environmental matters are at best uneven, with some regions and topics well covered by existing books and atlases, and other parts of Central Eurasia less well represented. It is thus the major purpose of this atlas to include maps on a wide variety of themes for all countries in our Central Eurasian region, from the Caucasus to Central Asia to Mongolia and China's three western provinces.

In making decisions on what topics to include in this atlas we looked at existing atlases and other sources for ideas we considered important in presenting topics about contemporary, not historical, Central Eurasia. We also decided to include maps on some topics not considered in existing sources that we believed were important in illustrating current economic, cultural, social, environmental and political problems and issues. For example, some historical maps were important, as they are important background materials to understand the present state of Central Eurasia. Other topics are "first time" topics in regional atlases, such as Internet cafés, gender index, environmental crises and geopolitical futures.

Following this brief introduction, the atlas continues with seven chapters (Chapters 2–8) entitled "General reference," "Historical," "Population," "Environment," "Economic," "Cultural" and "Political," each of which includes five to twelve maps about one or more facets of each topic. Chapter 9, entitled "Countries and provinces," presents basic historical, cultural, economic and political information; some of this is background information one would find in other sources, but we considered it important to material in this section. A base map of each country or Chinese province is included, as is a population pyramid. Chapter 10 is called "Central Eurasian scenarios"; it presents ten scenarios of what Central Eurasia might look like in the next fifty years. Added to the descriptions are six hypothetical maps of political realignment in the region, cartographies that are almost certain to stimulate some healthy scholarly debate and discussion. Finally, in the Bibliography, we list general and specific books, chapters and atlases that one might use to access further information about the region. A number of websites are included; many were used to construct maps for this atlas. The map symbols and language terms used throughout the atlas are shown in Table 1.

We believe this atlas of Central Eurasia serves four main purposes. First, it contains a greater variety and number of maps and graphics (more than a hundred) than any other current atlas. It is thus an important and unique addition to the scholarly literatures. Second, we envision its use in disciplinary and interdisciplinary classes and seminars focusing on Central Eurasia as well as workshops by governments, nongovernmental organizations (NGOs) and the private sector. These learning sessions might focus on one set of maps, for example, those on environmental issues, economic development or social well-being. Third, it will be a most useful source for scholars ferreting out research topics for theses or dissertations in the humanities and also the social, policy and environmental sciences. In our view, behind each map and map pattern is a series of questions through which one might inquire about both temporal and spatial processes that are worth unraveling through archival research and fieldwork. Fourth, the atlas will be a useful reference source for those working in libraries where reference questions about Central Eurasia will only increase in the coming years.

In our minds, Central Eurasia is a region that is becoming more important and increasingly recognized as an important geoeconomic, geopolitical, geocultural and geoenvironmental region. This "coming of age," as noted above, is very apparent in disciplinary and inter-disciplinary scholarly circles. It is also, to be sure, being recognized as crucial in European and Asian geoeconomic and geopolitical decisions by corporations, organizations and governments. For these groups and others, it is important to have a specialized atlas available that includes maps of many of the issues important to present and future generations of scholars, NGOs, governments and corporations.

Table 1 Map symbols and foreign terms

MAP SYMBOLS		FOREIGN TERMS	
Boundaries		Aylagy	gulf
		Co	lake
·-·—·—·--	International boundary	Dag	mountain
—·—·—·—	'State' boundary	Darya	river
····················	Provincial boundary (China)	Dasht	desert/plain
···············	Former oblast boundary	Gobi	rocky desert
		Gol	river
Transportation		Gum	lake
		Hai	lake/sea
·—+—+—+—··	Railroad	He	river
		Hu	lake
Water Features		Kel'	lake
		Köl	lake
∿	River/stream	Koli	lake
⊞⊞⊞⊞	Canal	Kul'	lake
▬	Sea/lake/reservoir	Kuli	lake
⬚	Salt pan/flat	Kum	sandy desert
···	Swamp/marsh	Kangri	mountain
▨	Glacier	Lich	lake
		Nu	lake
Physical Features		Nur	lake
		Nuur	lake
░	Desert	Ozero	lake
▱	Depression	Pendi	basin
		Qum	lake
Cultural Features		Qumy	lake
⊛ **Astana**	Country capital	Shamo	desert
⊙ Mary	'State' capital	Shan	mountain range
▪ Kerki	City/town	Tau	mountain
		Taw	mountain
BALKAN	'State'	Tou	mountain

2   General reference

Geographic grid

Scholars debate the geographical extent of the region studied in this atlas and also the term to best describe it. Eurasia could be considered as that large land mass that includes all territory east of the Urals, all the way to the northwest Pacific Ocean. Or it could encompass only the five countries in Central Asia: Kazakhstan, Kyrgyzstan, Tajikistan, Turkmenistan and Uzbekistan. This atlas includes these five states in Middle or Central Asia, but also the three states, all former Soviet republics, in the Caucasus, Armenia, Azerbaijan and Georgia, which many scholars writing about historical or contemporary events consider to have more in common culturally and politically with the Central Asian states than with Europe. Nevertheless, it is important to recognize that there remains a certain amount of ambiguity regarding the accepted territorial limits of what we term Central Eurasia.

The ambiguity in defining the western extent of Central Eurasia also occurs when attempting to establish an eastern boundary. In particular, questions surface over whether it is prudent to use the boundaries of existing states as the best way to delimit this region. If one uses only state and international political boundaries, one would probably exclude Mongolia and also the three westernmost provincial-level units of China, namely Tibet, Xinjiang and Qinghai. However, a very legitimate case can be made for including these units in Central Eurasia as their history and culture are tied closely to those of the five Central Asian states. Whether in terms of religion, language or cultural influences, the three Chinese administrative regions have more in common with Kazakhstan, Kyrgyzstan and Mongolia than they do with central and eastern China, whose pre- and post-colonial history is in sharp contrast.

Geographic location

This mid-latitude region of 9.3 million km^2 (3.6 million square miles) extends across roughly 80 degrees longitude (from 40° E to 120° E) and 30 degrees latitude (from 27° N to 55° N). It is bordered on the west by the small Caucasus state of Georgia, which is on the eastern side of the Black Sea, and on the east by the eastern extreme of Mongolia. Western Georgia lies at a similar latitude to Madagascar in the southern hemisphere and eastern Mongolia is roughly on the same longitude as Perth in Western Australia. Central Eurasia's northern hemisphere latitude is comparable to northern Florida and its northern extent comparable to Labrador or Alaska's Pacific coast archipelago. In a southern hemisphere context the area would be similar to a region stretching from South America's Southern Cone to the southern third of Australia.

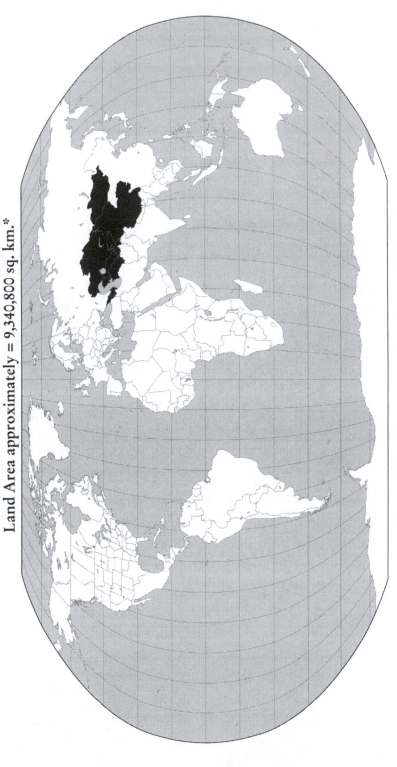

CENTRAL EURASIA'S GEOGRAPHIC LOCATION

Longitudinal extent: 40°E to 120°E
Latitudinal extent: 27°30'N to 55°30'N
Land Area approximately = 9,340,800 sq. km.*

*Land Area of Canada is approximately 9,100,000 sq. km.

Map 1 Central Eurasia's geographic location

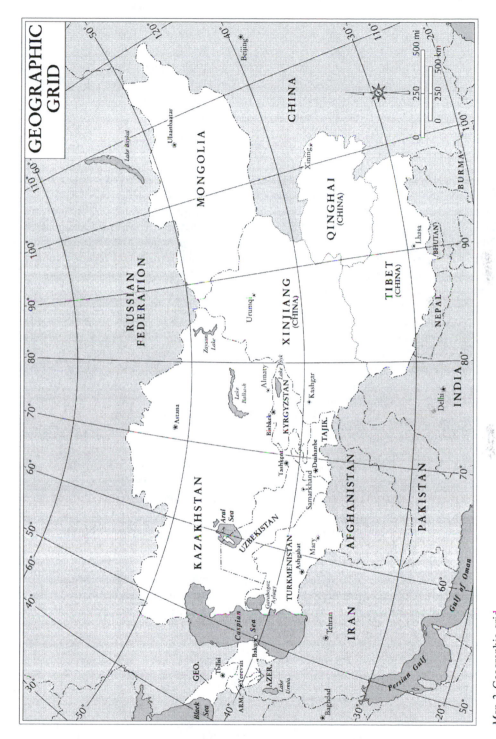

GEOGRAPHIC GRID

Map 2 Geographic grid

Regions and subregions

The territorial size of Central Eurasia is larger than the conterminous United States and roughly equal to that of the South American continent. If Central Eurasia were a country, it would be the fifth largest overall. It would still only be one-third the size of Russia, but it would be larger than Australia or Brazil. What makes this region distinctive on world maps is its interior location in the large Eurasian land mass. While some would define it as an area extending from the Urals all the way east to the Pacific Ocean, others would consider it a region more like the area we are using in this atlas.

Central Eurasia region

The region as we define it in this atlas includes nine states or countries and three Chinese provinces. The states include three in the Caucasus (Armenia, Azerbaijan and Georgia), five in Central Asia (Kazakhstan, Kyrgyzstan, Tajikistan, Turkmenistan and Uzbekistan) plus Mongolia. The provinces in western China, Tibet, Qinghai and Xinjiang, round out the Central Eurasian region. While Armenia, with an area of less than 30,000 km^2 (11,580 square miles), and Georgia, at 69,700 km^2 (approx. 26,900 square miles), are the smallest countries, the largest are Kazakhstan (approx. 2.7 million km^2 or 1 million square miles) and Mongolia (approx. 1.5 million km^2 or 604,000 square miles). The Xinjiang Autonomous Region (approx. 1.6 million km^2 or 640,000 square miles) is slightly larger than both Mongolia and the Tibet Autonomous Region (1.2 million km^2 or 474,162 square miles). All the Central Eurasian states except Mongolia and the three Chinese western provinces would fit into Kazakhstan; in fact, together they would fill only half of Kazakhstan's territory.

Aside from the vastly different population sizes of states in this region, a topic discussed below, there are two other distinctive features observed on the base map. One is the nature of the international boundaries. Five countries border southern Russia; two of them, Kazakhstan and Mongolia, have lengthy borders with this northern neighbor. China's border with Russia in Central Eurasia is very narrow, just a small piece of territory separating Kazakhstan and Mongolia. Most of these international border areas are lightly populated, but they are nonetheless very important in the world of contemporary geo-politics and economics. Two examples illustrate this point: the border between Georgia and Russia, which has been a seedbed of conflict, most recently in 2008, and the northern boundary of Kazakhstan, which is of cultural significance as it has a high density of Russians living especially in urban areas. There are also many Kazakhs in the border area of Xinjiang.

The second distinctive feature of Central Eurasia is that there is almost no access to open water, that is, these countries and provinces are landlocked. Western Georgia borders the Black Sea which feeds into the Mediterranean Sea which then flows into the eastern Atlantic. The Caspian Sea (or lake as some scholars label it) also has internal drainage, having no access to open waters. The landlocked status of this region is not an insignificant fact when one considers the transport networks with other countries and also the geopolitical role these countries play in regional economics and politics.

Mongolia and the west China subregion

The eastern portion of Central Eurasia includes the state of Mongolia as well as China's three western provinces. Western China is at the transition zone of Outer China and Inner

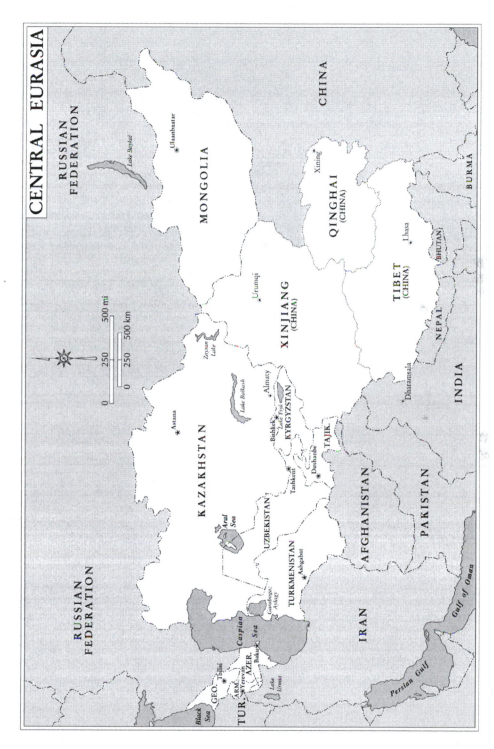

Map 3 Central Eurasia

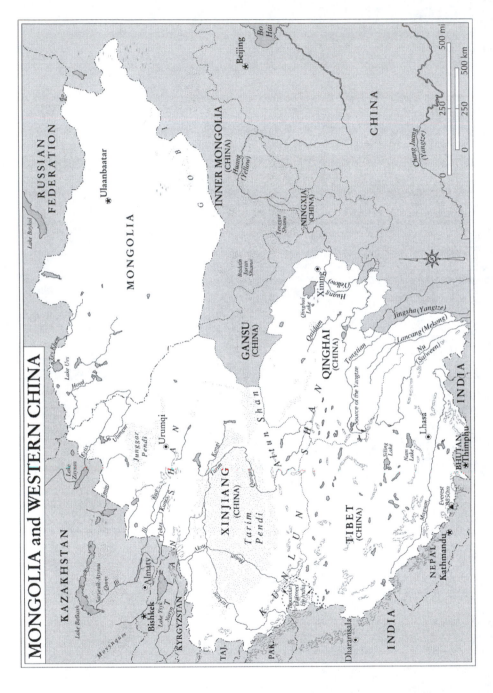

Map 4 Mongolia and western China

Asia, which includes the Xinjiang Uyghur Autonomous Region, the Tibet Autonomous Region and Qinghai Province. The Inner Mongolian Autonomous Region is related as well, but much of that land is well integrated into China (much of the population is Han Chinese), while in Xinjiang, Qinghai and Tibet, much of the population is Uyghur or Tibetan. Islam is common among Hui, Uyghur and Kazakh peoples, while the Tibetans and Mongols traditionally follow Lama Buddhism. The cultural and historical geographies of the peoples in western China and Mongolia link well with those of the peoples of Central Asia in the former Soviet Union.

Mongolia, independent since 1921, is a large landlocked state between China and Russia. There are three subregions: (1) the northern steppe area around Ulaanbaatar, (2) the western area around the Altay Mountains and (3) the southern areas around the Gobi Desert.

The Xinjiang Uyghur Autonomous Region is China's largest territorial unit. The Tian Shan (Heavenly Mountains) divide the region. There are four parts: (1) the central area around Urumqi, (2) the area north of the Tian Shan around the Junggar Basin, (3) the eastern area around the Turpan Basin and (4) the southern region around the Tarim Basin. South of the Kunlun Range lies Tibet.

The Tibet (Xizang) Autonomous Region lies high on the plateau at the roof of the world. There are three parts: (1) the north and western areas with many lakes, called by the Tibetans the Chang Tang or northern plateau, (2) the south with many rivers, particularly the Yarlung which becomes the Brahmaputra in India and (3) the eastern border with Sichuan (which also has Tibetan people). The first two subregions are part of the cultural region known as U-Tsang to the Tibetans, while they know the third as Kham.

Qinghai, a separate province in western China, lies on the Tibetan Plateau. It has three parts: (1) the eastern area around Qinghai Lake and Xining, (2) the northern area of the Qaidam Basin and (3) the southern area of mountains which are the source of the Yellow (Huang He) and Yangtze (Chang) rivers. Tibetans know this cultural region as Amdo.

Central Asia subregion

Central Asia includes the countries of Kazakhstan, Kyrgyzstan, Uzbekistan, Turkmenistan and Tajikistan. With the exception of the Tajiks and Russians, all of the main ethnic groups in this subregion are Turk. These five states were all republics in the former Soviet Union, which referred to Middle Asia (Srednaya Aziya) as consisting of Kyrgyzstan, Uzbekistan, Turkmenistan and Tajikistan. After independence in 1990, representatives of the former Soviet Central Asian republics met in Tashkent and decided to include Kazakhstan in their contemporary definition of Central Asia (Tsentralnaya Aziya). The five states are also known as the "stans," "stan" meaning "place of" in Persian. Russia lies to the north of Central Asia, the Caspian Sea and Caucasus to the west, Iran and Afghanistan to the south, and China to the east. Central Asia as a whole is mostly Islamic (although there are substantial Russian minorities in Kazakhstan), has gas and oil reserves and a long history dating back before the Silk Road.

Kazakhstan, the world's largest landlocked country, has four parts: (1) the Kazakh uplands (steppe) in the north, (2) the western areas between the Caspian and the Aral Sea, (3) the eastern area around the Ili Valley and Lake Balkash (Almaty is located near here), and (4) the southern areas around the Syr Darya.

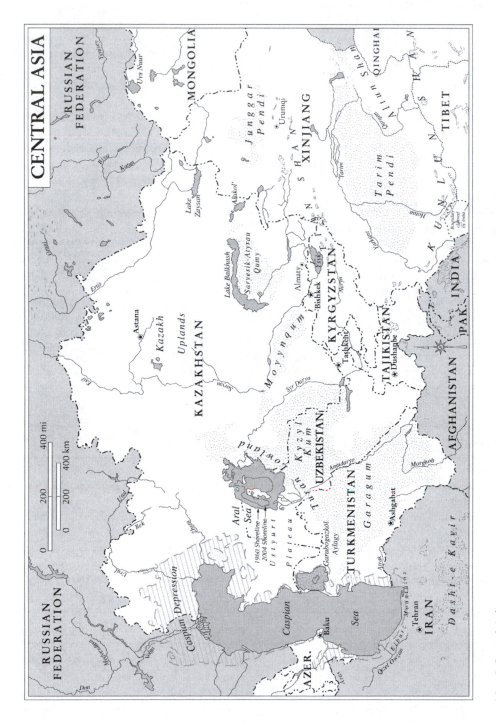

Map 5 Central Asia

Kyrgyzstan is very mountainous; the Tian Shan (Tenghri Tagh, or Heavenly Mountains) account for 80 percent of the country. It has four parts: (1) the northern core around Bishkek, (2) the east around Ysyk Köl (Warm Lake), (3) the western areas around Osh in the Fergana Valley and (4) the southern mountainous areas on the border with China and Tajikistan.

Uzbekistan, the most populous country in Central Asia, is doubly landlocked, that is, a person from Uzbekistan must cross two countries to reach the ocean, and it borders all the other Central Asian countries. There are four parts: (1) the Fergana Valley in the east, (2) the northern core around Tashkent, (3) the south-central historical centers around Samarkhand and Bukhara, and (4) the western areas of the Kyzyl Kum (desert), Turan lowland and Ustyurt Plateau.

Turkmenistan is 80 percent covered by the Garagum (Black Sand) Desert. It has four parts: (1) the north along the Amu Darya, (2) the central with the Garagum Desert, (3) the south with Ashgabat and (4) the west along the Caspian Sea.

Tajikistan is landlocked, mountainous and the smallest of the Central Asian countries. It has four physical regions: (1) the central core around Dushanbe, (2) the northern area around the Fergana Valley, (3) the southern area on the border with Afghanistan and (4) the eastern area which consists mostly of the Pamir Mountains.

Caucasus subregion

The Caucasus subregion comprises the western segment of Central Eurasia. Named after and just to the south of the Caucasus Mountains, this subregion consists of Georgia, Armenia and Azerbaijan. Another name for the three countries is the Transcaucasus. We are not discussing the area north of the Caucasus in Russia which includes Chechnya and Dagestan. The northern border of this subregion is the Caucasus Mountains and Russia, the western border is the Black Sea and Turkey, the eastern border is the Caspian Sea and the southern border is Iran. Georgia, Armenia and Azerbaijan speak different languages. While Georgia and Armenia have a Christian heritage, Azerbaijan is Muslim. While these countries are not members of the European Union, most post-Soviet geographies point toward the Caucasus subregion as being in Europe rather than Asia or the Middle East. In this context the Caucasus subregion is the European portion of Central Eurasia.

Georgia (in its language, Sakartvelo) is relatively mountainous. The country has three parts: (1) the northern areas along the Caucasus Mountains, including the areas of Abkhazia and South Ossetia which have claimed independence (note: they are not recognized by Georgia and the vast majority of states), (2) the western areas on the Black Sea (known as Colchis) and (3) the eastern areas around Tbilisi (known as Iberia).

Armenia (in its language, Hayastan) is mountainous and landlocked, with Turkey to the west, Georgia to the north, Azerbaijan to the east and Iran to the south. There are two subregions divided by the Lesser Caucasus: (1) the northern areas around Yerevan and Lake Sevana, and (2) the southern areas, which are situated between the western and eastern portions of Azerbaijan.

Azerbaijan is the largest of the states in the Caucasus. It is landlocked, but has access to the Caspian Sea. There are four physical regions in Azerbaijan: (1) the eastern areas along the Caspian Sea around Baku, (2) the northern areas along the Caucasus, (3) the central plain in the interior, including the formerly autonomous oblast of Nagorno-Karabakh, and (4) the western exclave of Naxçivan to the west of southern Armenia.

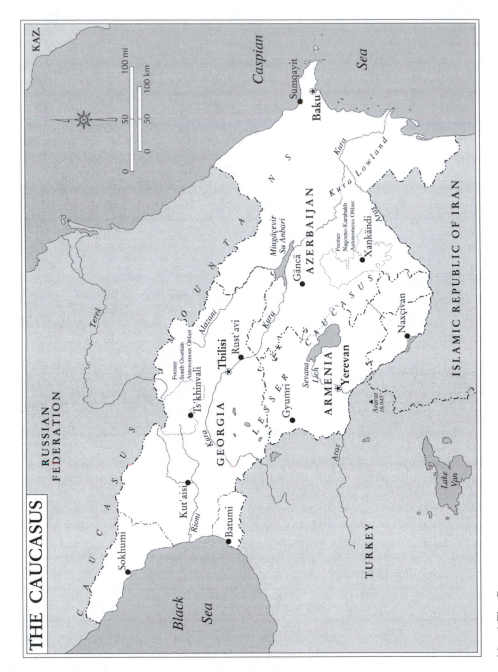

Map 6 The Caucasus

3 Historical

Early Turkic Empire: sixth to seventh century CE

From their origins in southern Siberia in the third to fourth century CE Nomadic Turk peoples began developing into a power in Central Eurasia when they migrated into Mongolia. In the fifth century, Turk nomads continued toward China and then westward into what is present-day Uzbekistan. (These Turk groups continued their westward migration, so that today Turk-speaking peoples have settled from Siberia to Turkey, including Uyghurs, Kazakhs, Uzbeks, Turkmen, Azeri and Turks.) By the sixth century, the Turk nomads united under the rule of the Göktürk confederation ("Blue" or "Celestial" Turk). As Turks continued their move westward, they controlled the Silk Road trade and became a major power in Central Eurasia. Originally Shamanistic, Turks added Buddhism, Manicheanism and Nestorian Christianity to their religious beliefs before settling on Islam.

The Turk Khanate had a series of confrontations to the south with the Chinese dynasties. By the early sixth century the Khanate had expanded into Uzbekistan and confronted the Hephthalites. By the latter part of the century internal conflict led to a division between the Western and Eastern Turk Khanates. The Eastern Turk Khanate alternately fought and allied with Chinese dynasties, while the Western Turk Khanate was fighting with the Hephthalites and the Sassanids. By 740 the Eastern Turk Khanate had had a series of wars with and been absorbed by Tang China. The Western Turk Khanate lasted a little longer as it allied with the Byzantines against the Sassanids. However, these conflicts weakened the Western Turk Khanate as it was caught between a new force to the west, the Arabs, and the pressures in the east from a rising Tang China.

Tang Dynasty China (618–907) occupied a great territory. The capital of the empire was Chang'an (modern-day Xi'an). Tang was a great cosmopolitan power with many traders from Central Asia coming to Chang'an. Religion expanded as well. Buddhism came from India to Afghanistan and Central Asia and to China by the third century. The Tang had its homelands on the Yellow and Yangtze rivers and expanded into Central Eurasia by 700. Tang used Turk peoples in service as mercenaries and as generals to aid in the expansion.

Tibet (from Bö in the indigenous language) developed into the Tibetan Empire from 608 to 842. Bon remained the main religion in the area until Buddhism entered from Nepal in the seventh century. Tibet had conflicts with Tang China from the seventh century through 800, although in general the high plateau remained under Tibetan control. The Tibetan Empire at times influenced trade along the southern Silk Road.

The Hephthalites were probably a mixed group of Turkic and proto-Iranian peoples originating in modern-day northwest India and Iran. They were Buddhist. By the fifth

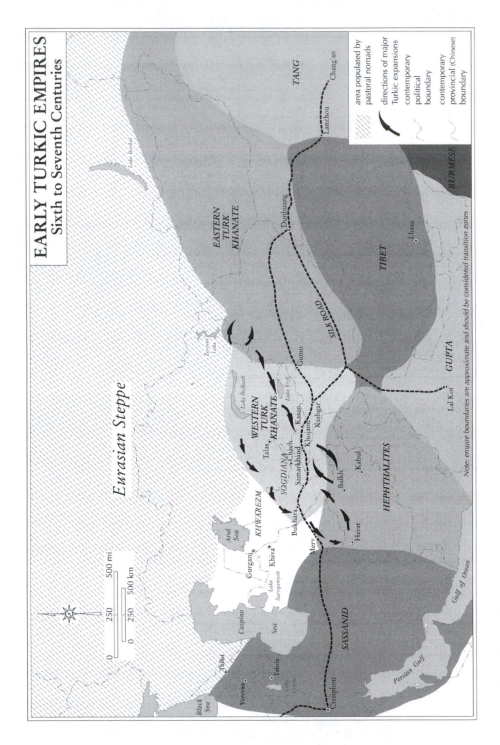

Map 7 Early Turkic Empires: sixth to seventh centuries

century they controlled Sogdiana and into Persia. Their base shifted into modern-day Afghanistan, which they controlled until the mid-sixth century.

The Sassanid Dynasty was one of the main Persian empires lasting from 224 when they succeeded the Parthians through the mid-seventh century. Their capital was at Ctesiphon which is near modern-day Baghdad. Their language was Persian, their religion Zoroastrianism and their cultural influence was very strong over the Silk Road. By 600 the Sassanids controlled an area east to Bactria and west to the Mediterranean where they were in conflict with the Western Turk Khanate, the Byzantines and the Hephthalites.

Khwarezm refers to the area around the delta of the Amu Darya, south of the Aral Sea. This area was settled by Iranian peoples and was for a time under Hephthalite and then Sassanid control.

This period saw the rise of the Turk khanates in Central Asia and was also marked by conflict between the Turk and Tang China in the east and the Turk and Sassanid Persia in the west. Central Eurasia became a region ethnically dominated by Turk-speaking peoples. Tibet was well established. Persians to the west and Chinese to the east influenced the region's culture and trade.

Arab conquest: eighth century

The Arab Omayyad (Umayyad) Caliphate (661–750) was the new power to influence Central Eurasia. Its capital was in Damascus, but the religious center was in Mecca. With the new religion of Islam, the caliphate extended into Persia and defeated the Sassanids by the mid-seventh century. By the latter part of the century the Arabs extended from Persia into Maveranahr. Maveranahr is the Arabic word for the Land beyond the River, in this case the Amu Darya. The Latin name is Transoxiana after the Oxus (Amu Darya). Not only did the Arabs conquer these areas, but many Persians and Turks converted to Islam as well. Thus the cultural and political fabric of Central Asia was being oriented to Mecca. In the late seventh century the Western Turk Khanate was fighting a losing battle against the Arab Omayyads and the converted populace. The Abbassids succeeded the Omayyads in 750 and reigned until 1258; their capital was in Baghdad.

China, under the Tang Dynasty, began to expand into Central Asia. Chang'an was a cosmopolitan city with Turk soldiers and Sogdian traders as well as a Chinese populace. Buddhism and then Islam both came along the Silk Road into China. Expansion into the Tarim Basin in the eighth century overtook the Eastern Turk Khanate. The Tang expanded beyond the Tian Shan and in 751 fought the battle of Talas (in modern Kyrgyzstan). In this conflict the Tang had a Korean general and Turk mercenaries, and they were aligned against the Arabs (by this time the new Abbasid Caliphate) and Tibetans, who also employed mercenaries, in this case Karluk Turks. By the end of the battle, few of the Tang forces survived and many were then made prisoners of war by the Arabs. Chinese artisans (in particular, those skilled in paper making) were brought to Baghdad. Much of the region became Islamic and the Tang were forced back into the Tarim.

The Tibetans continued their conflicts with the Tang Dynasty though to 820. They controlled much of the plateau with their capital in Lhasa. Tibet remains Buddhist. With the battle of Talas and the retreat of the Tang, Tibet exerted more influence over the southern Silk Road. The boundaries between Tang China and Tibet were established in a peace treaty in 821.

Another Turkic group, the Uyghur, replaced the Eastern Turk Khanate from 745 to 840, with their center in Ordu Baliq in Mongolia. Many Uyghurs migrated to Karakhoja and

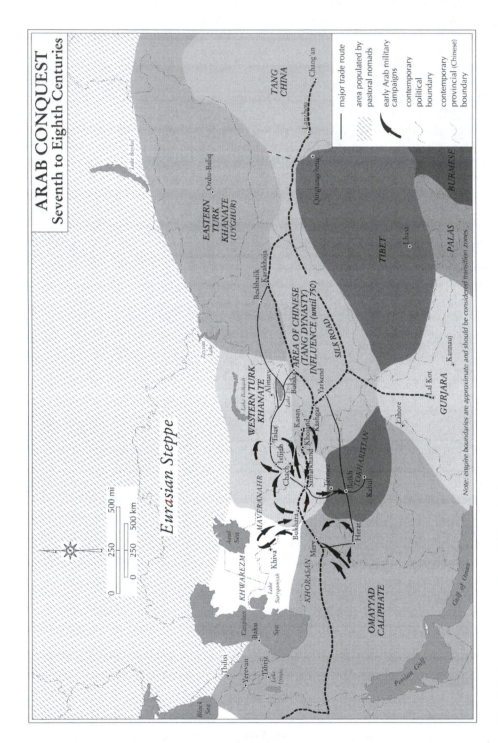

Map 8 Arab conquest: seventh to eighth centuries

Beshbalik (in modern-day Xinjiang) and ruled there from 850 to 1209. At first the Uyghurs in the north were Shamanistic, but later in Karakhoja, the Uyghur followed Buddhism, Manicheanism and Nestorian Christianity.

During this period, the Arab caliphates overtook Persia, but more importantly, Islam became dominant in western areas of the Central Eurasian region, supplanting Buddhism. The Chinese Tang Dynasty first expanded and then contracted. Variants of Buddhism became the dominant belief system in Tang China, Tibet and the Uyghur Khanate.

Mongol rule: thirteenth century

After the Turks and the Arabs, another power had a great impact on Central Eurasia, namely the Mongols. Genghis Khan unified the Mongol tribes by 1206 and, through superior warfare, especially using mounted bowmen, by 1221 the Mongols had become the only power to conquer and rule all of Central Eurasia, China and Persia. While the Mongols did not populate Central Eurasia, their rule was marked by a vast transcontinental trade and cultural exchange, with communications flowing both from west to east and east to west. The Venetian merchant Marco Polo and the Flemish Franciscan William of Rubruck traveled from Europe to China, while the Nestorian Turk monk Rabban Bar Sauma traveled from China to Baghdad and Rome. Mongol rulers utilized Uyghurs, Turks and Persians in their dominion over China and Central Eurasia and by the end of their rule, there was a continued Turkization of Mongol society. Much of the population of the western Khanates (Batu, Hulegu and Chagatai) was Muslim and there was rapid growth in trade under Pax Mongolica.

After the death of Genghis Khan in 1227, the empire divided into four great hordes, or Ulus: (1) the Ulus of the Great Khan (Yuan) over China, (2) the Ulus of Chagatai from the Tarim Basin to the Amu Darya, (3) the Ulus of Jochi (Batu) from Lake Balkash to the Black Sea, and (4) the Ulus of Hulegu (the Il-Khanate) over Persia through Arabia. The Ulus of the Great Khan was centered in Karakorum. Kublai Khan moved the center to Dadu (modern Beijing), establishing the Yuan Dynasty in China (1271–1368). The Ulus of Chagatai was centered in Almalik in the Ili River valley. The Chagatai Khanate lost its western holdings to the Timurid Empire in 1369–1404, but continued to hold the Tarim and Ili valleys till 1687. The Ulus of Jochi (Batu) (1240–1480) was centered in Sarai on the Volga. This Ulus became known as the Golden Horde, controlling Russia and attacking Poland and Hungary. The Ulus of Hulegu (1256–1335), centered in Tabriz, succeeded the Abbasids in control over Persia and stretched from Afghanistan to Turkey. The Timurid Dynasty (1370–1526) succeeded in controlling lands from Hulegu, the Golden Horde and Chagatai Ulus.

Colonial powers: eighteenth century

In the aftermath of the Timurids, new states conquered the area. The eighteenth century saw continuing powers in Central Eurasia and also the rise of new powers. Russia was one of the latter, centered in Moscow and conquering khanates along the Volga River by 1600. Under Peter the Great (1682–1725), the Russian Empire expanded eastward into Siberia. Another new power, the Manchu, conquered Mongolia, China, Tibet (1720) and East Turkistan (1750), founding the Qing Dynasty (1644–1911). Manchu power was centered first in Manchuria and then Beijing.

In the heart of Central Eurasia the Bukharans, Khivans, Kazakhs and Turkomans held sway. The Bukharan Khanate ruled from 1500 to 1785, and was succeeded by the Bukharan

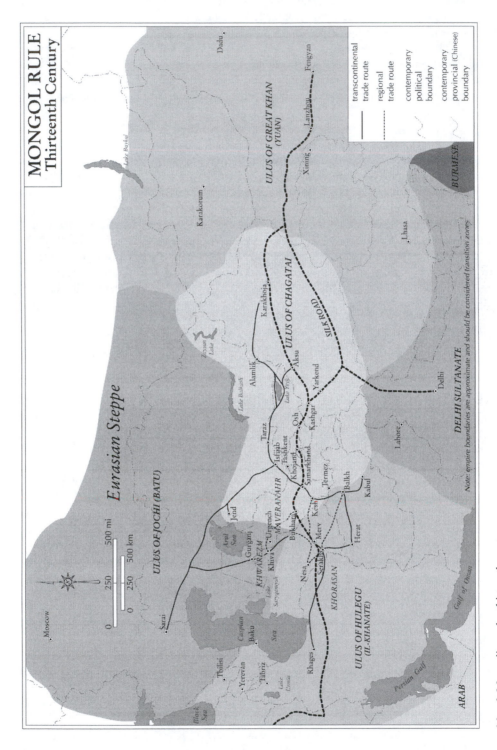

Map 9 Mongolian rule: thirteenth century

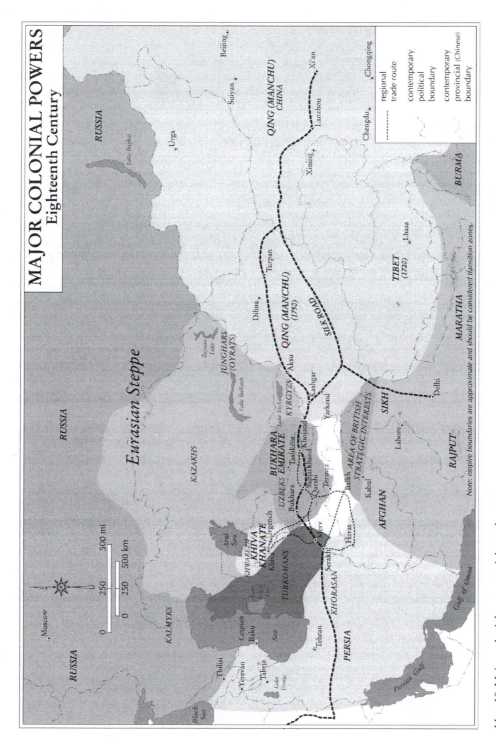

Map 10 Major colonial powers: eighteenth century

Emirate (1785–1920). Its peoples included Uzbeks and Persians. The Khivan Khanate (1511–1920) was centered on the Amu Darya, with much of its population Uzbek. The Russian tsars conquered Khiva and Bukhara in 1873. The Kazakhs were descendants of Turks, Mongols and Eurasians. The Kazakh Khanate (1465–1847) was formed from remnants of the Golden Horde. By 1718 this khanate was composed of three *jüz* (clans), the Great, Middle and Lesser Jüz of Kazakhs. The Kazakhs were fighting the Junghar (Oyrat) Mongols to their east. The Russian Empire began to expand into the region, absorbing the Lesser Jüz in 1731, the Middle in 1798, and the Great Jüz in 1820. The Turkomans were descendants of Turk peoples who had migrated south of the Amu Darya and were an independent tribal confederation after the collapse of the Timurid Empire. The Russian Empire expanded into Turkoman lands in 1869 and controlled the areas by 1894.

In India, the rulers of the Mughal Empire (1526–1858) were descendants of the Timurids. These Muslim rulers initially spoke Chagatai (the first ruler, Babur, was from the Fergana Valley) and then Persian and Urdu. By 1700 the empire was beginning to fall apart, with the Maratha (1674–1820) in central India, the Afghan (Durrani) Empire (1747–1826), the Sikhs (1799–1849) in Punjab and British colonialism all contributing to its dissolution. The British Empire became a new power in Central Eurasia, expanding from its foothold in India. The East India Company first operated there in 1612, and by 1757 Company rule was established in Bengal. The British Raj existed from 1858 to 1947. India included areas administered by the British crown as well as princely states. By the latter part of the eighteenth century British strategic interests had moved toward Afghanistan and Tibet.

In Persia the Safavid (1501–1736), the Afsharid (1736–96), the Zand (1750–94) and the Qajar dynasties (1785–1925) ruled. The Safavids had conflicts with the Ottomans and the Uzbeks and the Afsharid controlled the largest Persian state since the Sassanids. The Zand had a peaceful and prosperous state during their short rule. The Qajars centered their power in Tehran and found themselves in conflict with the Russians as the latter marched south. Britain also became interested in Persia.

This period of colonial control marked the entry of new powers (Russian, British and Manchu) into Central Eurasia. These new powers took over lands from older ones – the Manchu in China, the Russians in the Central Asian khanates and the British in India. Meanwhile the people of Central Eurasia were mostly Turks and Muslims in the western areas, while the eastern areas had Tibetans and Mongols who were mostly Buddhist.

The Great Game or Tournament of Shadows (1813–1907) marks the rivalry between Russia and Britain over Central Eurasia. Britain wished to retain its empire in India while the Russian Empire was moving southward into Central Eurasia. The Manchu Qing Empire had also expanded into Central Eurasia by 1750.

The Silk Road

The Silk Road was an amalgam of overland trade routes that traversed Central Eurasia. The German geographer Ferdinand von Richtofen coined the term *Seidenstraße* in 1877. Besides silk, other possible appellations include horse, amber, alfalfa, grape, furs, jewels, spices or rhubarb. All were traded on the routes of the Silk Road. The term Silk Road in truth is a modern invention to describe a rather old trade route. The roads taken were around deserts and over mountain passes from the Mediterranean to Asia. Most merchants only traversed a portion of the route; very few traveled from end to end. Besides products, technologies were also transferred, such as those of printing and weaving, of glass making and cartography. Cultural transmissions also include religions (Buddhism and Islam) and

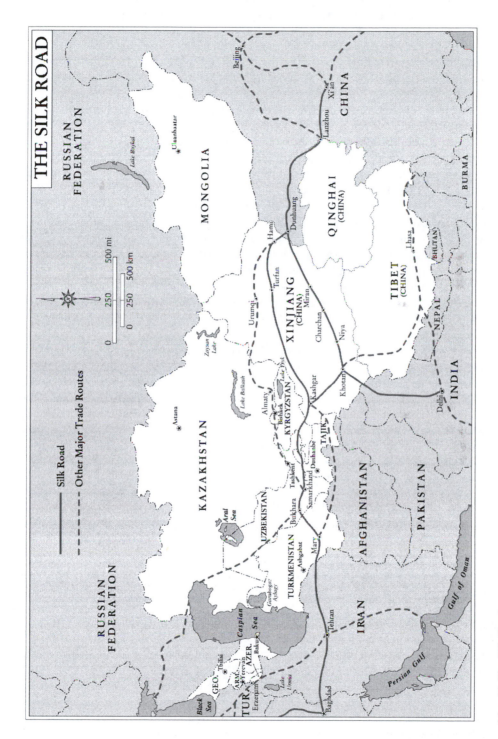

Map 11 The Silk Road

languages (Greek, Turk, Persian, Chinese and Mongol to name a few). Buddhism spread from India to Afghanistan and Tibet, to Central Asia and to China, and Islam spread from Arabia to Persia and Central Asia, to India and China, both along the Silk Road. People spread their religion, languages, technology and cultures, but they also migrated themselves. One great migration was of the Turk peoples westward from Mongolia to Turkey. Chinese peoples migrated westward but not as far. Persians migrated eastward and Russians migrated southward.

The highpoints of trade along the Silk Road occurred in four periods: (1) Rome, Parthian and Han, (2) Byzantine, Turk and Tang, (3) Mongol and (4) modern. Between 200 BCE and 200 CE, Rome and Han China did not have direct contact with one another, but certainly silk produced in China made its way westward to Rome through intermediaries such as Parthia and the Xiongnu nomads of the Central Eurasian steppe. Between 600 and 900 CE trade linking Byzantium and Tang China was through intermediaries such as the Turks, Persians and Arabs. From 1200 to 1400 the Mongols controlled the land from China to the Mediterranean, thus making trade much easier. By the 1500s the sea routes between Europe and Asia came more into use, so the overland trade from end to end lessened. By the 1800s the Great Game had supplanted the Silk Road, with British, Persian, Russian and Chinese empires contending for power in Central Eurasia.

Who traveled this road? The works of Marco Polo are well known, even if his authenticity is sometimes questioned. Polo traveled the Silk Road from 1272 to 1295 going to see the Great Khan in Khan Baliq (Beijing) via the Il-khanate in Persia and the Chagatai Khanate in the Tarim Basin.

Who are some of the less well-known travelers on the Silk Road? Zhang Qian, Chinese emissary to Central Asia 138–125 BCE, was seeking an alliance between the Han Dynasty and the Yuezhi against the Xiongnu. While the alliance was not successful, Zhang Qian did travel from Chang'an (Xi'an) to the Tarim Basin, Fergana Valley, Bactria (Afghanistan) and Sogdiana (Uzbekistan) and brought this knowledge back to the Han court.

Xuan Zang, a Chinese monk (602–64 CE), went on a pilgrimage to India to gather Buddhist scriptures. In 629 he traveled from Chang'an (Xi'an) to Turfan, Lake Ysyk, Chach (Tashkent), Samarkhand, Balkh and Bamiyan (Afghanistan), and thence to India. After studying there for several years, he returned to China by way of Kashgar, Hotan and Dunhuang in 645 CE. His work, *Great Tang Records on the Western Regions*, describes in detail the geography of Central and South Asia. He translated many Buddhist scriptures from Sanskrit to Chinese and thus was instrumental in the transmission of Buddhism to China.

Sogdian merchants in the eighth century traveled from Samarkhand, Sogdiana (Uzbekistan) to Chang'an (Xi'an) across the Tian Shan range and around the Taklamakan Desert via Kashgar and Dunhuang. Letters from Sogdian merchants profile the commodities traded along the Silk Road, including silver, linen, pepper, musk and lead powder. Sogdians and other merchants also spread Manicheanism and Buddhism along the route.

William of Rubruck, a Flemish Franciscan monk, traveled from Constantinople to Karakorum in 1253 to gain an audience with the Mongol Khan to promote Christianity. He journeyed across the Black Sea, to Sarai on the Volga, across the steppe to Mongolia. From his writings we gain knowledge of the Golden Horde (the Ulus of Batu), as well as of daily life among the Mongols, nomad life in the steppe and the Mongol court at Karakorum.

Rabban Bar Sauma, a Turk, was a Nestorian monk born near Khan Baliq (Beijing) in 1220. In 1275 he set off on a pilgrimage to Jerusalem but made it only as far as Baghdad. He traveled to Hotan, Kashgar, Talas, Khorasan and Mosul on his way to Baghdad, passing through the Chagatai and Hulegu khanates. From Baghdad he was sent by the Mongol Arghun Khan in 1287 as emissary to the Byzantines, the Pope and European royalty, seeking an alliance against the Mamluk (Arab followers of Islam). His records, *The Life and Travels of Rabban Sawma to Constantinople, Rome, France, and back to Baghdad*, of 1288 provide excellent observations on medieval Europe and Central Eurasia from a Turk/Mongol/ Nestorian perspective.

Merchants, mercenaries and monks all trod this Silk Road, just as modern times tourists follow in their footsteps. Today the Silk Road is much easier to travel. Whether flying from Beijing to Urumqi, Moscow to Bishkek, Istanbul to Tashkent, crossing the Khunjerab or Torugart passes by bus or taking the train from China to Kazakhstan and on to Russia, we all can travel the Silk Road too.

4 Population

Three features stand out clearly on maps depicting population densities in the Caucasus, Central Asia, Mongolia and western China: extremely low densities, vast areas throughout the region with very few or no inhabitants, and the high population densities around major urban, administrative and industrial centers.

Low densities mark most of western China, Mongolia and Central Asia, especially Kazakhstan, Uzbekistan and Turkmenistan. These are areas of extremely inhospitable climates for any sustainable and highly productive agriculture; they include regions with some of the greatest extremes of temperature on the planet and also those with little or no precipitation. The "islands" of higher densities in Mongolia, western China and Central Asia are mostly capital cities and industrial regions or associated with some productive land resource, such as a mineral or an energy source or irrigated agriculture. One can easily pick out Ulaanbaatar, Mongolia, Xining, Urumqi and Lhasa in western China as well as Almaty (former capital of Kazakhstan), Bishkek, Tashkent, Dushanbe and Ashgabat, all capitals today except Almaty. Kazakhstan moved its capital to Astana in northern Kazakhstan in 1997.

Two areas of high population density in Central Asia are the extremely productive Fergana Valley in southern Kyrgyzstan and adjacent Uzbekistan, which is important for growing fruits and vegetables for large and small urban markets in the region, and the borderlands of northern Kazakhstan and southern Russia. In this latter region there reside today, as they have for centuries, large concentrations of Russians and Kazakhs in both the rural areas and cities. During Soviet years the cities of Pavlodar, Semey (formerly Semipalatinsk) and Ust-Kamenogorsk (also known as Oskemen today) were major industrial cities, along with Karaganda (south of Astana), Aktau and Atyrau (on the northeast shore of the Caspian Sea).

The population densities are much higher in the Caucasus region than elsewhere in Central Eurasia. They are higher because they are associated with highly successful and productive mineral and agricultural economies. It is not only the capital cities that have high densities, but also middle-sized industrial areas. The regions provide food and industrial products not only to former Soviet republics, which are their neighbors, but also to other nearby countries in Europe and southwest Asia.

Population density

Mongolia and west China

The dominant feature of these three provinces plus Mongolia is their extremely low population density. Almost half the area has fewer than 2.5 persons per square mile (6.4 per km^2).

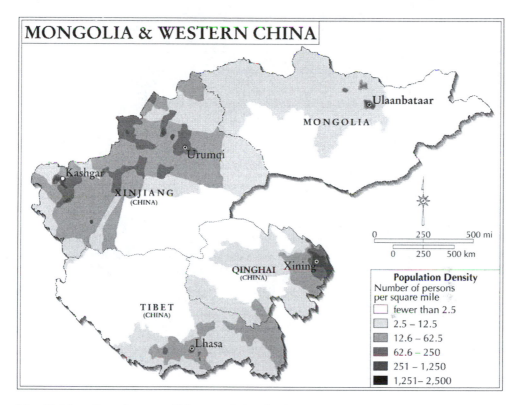

Map 12 Mongolia and western China: population density

This region includes southern and eastern Mongolia, southeastern Xinjiang, northern and western Qinghai and the western half of Tibet. Almost another third of the area has 2.5–10 persons per square mile (6.4–26 per km²). One associates these low density areas not only with few residents but also with extremely harsh environments: very hot, very cold, little precipitation and inhospitable terrain for intensive productive agriculture. Many of these sparsely populated areas have little or no economic activity or economic livelihoods tied to nomadic economies, especially livestock herding.

The few areas of high population density are provincial cities (Urumqi, Xining and Lhasa), a capital city (Ulaanbaatar), and regions associated with productive economic agricultural and mining activities along river valleys (southern Tibet) and near major highway and rail connections (western Xinjiang) and industrial centers (Urumqi and Xining). These high-density nodes are in sharp contrast to the vast "seas" of low density around them. Population in Xinjiang follows the roads and railroads from Urumqi. One route lies west from Urumqi to Shihezi, Karamay and to Gulja (Yining). The other route lies to the south from Urumqi to Turpan, Korla and Aksu and west to Kashgar. In Tibet, Lhasa and Shigatse are the major centers, while in Qinghai, these are Xining and Haidong.

Central Asia

The variations in population density in this region are attributed to the contrast between places with productive agricultural and industrial economies and those that comprise vast

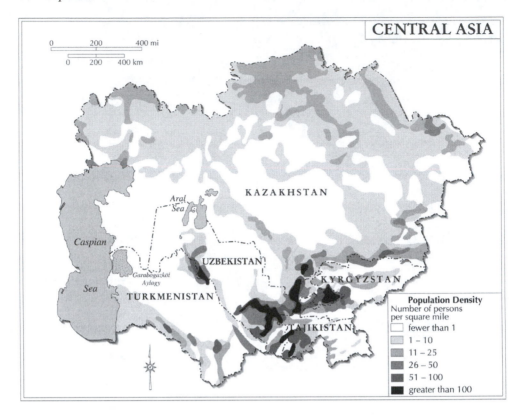

Map 13 Central Asia: population density

areas of harsh environmental conditions. Less than 10 percent of the region has a population density exceeding 100 persons per square mile (259 per km²). These areas include the very productive and irrigated Fergana Valley in southern Kyrgyzstan and eastern and southern Uzbekistan and various administrative and industrial centers. Immediately adjacent to many of these high-density nodes and regions are vast areas of very rugged terrain and desert-like conditions which are generally unproductive. Examples of these harsh areas are most of Turkmenistan and much of Uzbekistan, central and western Kazakhstan (all contain vast areas of deserts), and the very rugged mountainous parts of eastern Tajikistan (the Pamirs) and Kyrgyzstan (the Tian Shan). Moderate densities (11–50 persons per square mile, 4.2–19.3 per km²) are found in productive river valleys, including parts of the lower Amu Darya in western Uzbekistan and river valleys between Almaty and Bishkek. River valleys in northeastern and north-central Kazakhstan (near Ust-Kamenogorsk (Oskemen) and Semey) have higher population densities because of good soils and major industrial centers. Farther west in northern Kazakhstan the moderate population densities are associated with the Virgin Lands Program which began five decades ago and aimed to bring the steppes under the plow. In extreme western Kazakhstan, especially near the Caspian Sea, the densities are as low as in central Kazakhstan and Turkmenistan, except the higher density node at the north end of the sea; here Atyrau with its oil and gas economies and banking functions stands out like an urban-industrial island in a vast desert.

Caucasus

In this set of three population density maps, the Caucasus has by far the highest population density. There are no large areas of low or moderate density on the scale that one observes in the provinces of western China and Mongolia as well as much of Central Asia. The high densities in Armenia, Azerbaijan and Georgia indicate highly productive agricultural and mining and industrial regions as well as capital cities and tourist economies (especially Georgia's Black Sea coast with the cities of P'oti and Batumi). Baku's oil and gas refineries and associated petrochemical industries contribute to its high density as well as representing the major political and cultural center of Azerbaijan. Yerevan and Tbilisi also are islands of high density. The productive river valleys extending in a southeasterly direction from western Georgia to central Azerbaijan are used for extensive production of fresh fruits and vegetables for nearby as well as distant markets.

As other maps in the atlas reveal, these high population densities are also associated with highly diverse linguistic and religious landscapes. Cultural diversity is a key feature of this region's human geography.

Human Development Index

The Human Development Index, developed by the United Nations Development Program (UNDP), is used by scholars and members of intergovernmental and nongovernmental organizations to compare quality of life and living standards. Periodic UN reports provide a comparative snapshot of these measures for nearly two hundred countries. The index is

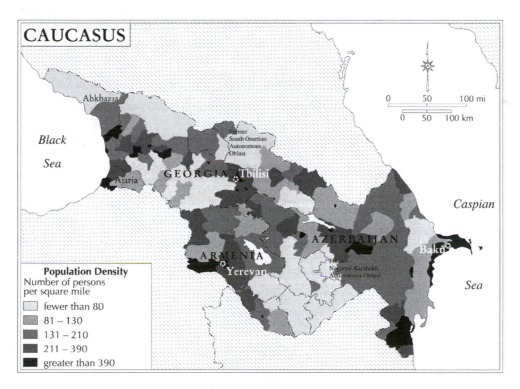

Map 14 Caucasus: population density

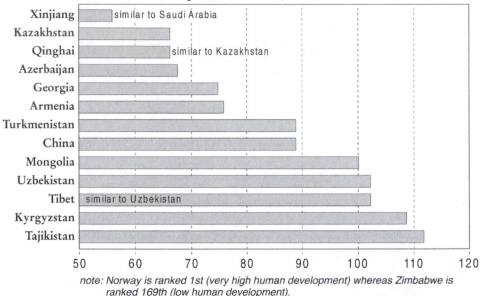

Human Development Index (HDI)-Rank

note: Norway is ranked 1st (very high human development) whereas Zimbabwe is
ranked 169th (low human development).

Figure 1 Human Development Index (HDI)

based on a number of criteria: life expectancy at birth, mean years of schooling (for adults), GNI (gross national income) per capita, inequality, poverty, gender, sustainability and human security. Data are published on both the composite index for each country as well as international rankings. The highest HDI rankings are for countries in northern and western Europe.

Rankings are provided for all countries in Central Eurasia. The highest were for Kazakhstan (ranked 66) and Armenia (ranked 67) and the lowest were for Uzbekistan (102) and Tajikistan (112). All other Central Eurasian countries were ranked between these groups. In general, Kazakhstan is ranked more highly owing to its oil economy which raises the GNI per capita. The Caucasus countries all rank below Kazakhstan and above the other Central Eurasian countries.

China's ranking was 89 which was almost the same as that of Turkmenistan. UNDP has also made assessments in China using the Human Development Index. When the Index variables are considered for Qinghai, Tibet and Xinjiang, these provinces rank at a similar level to Saudi Arabia, Kazakhstan and Uzbekistan respectively.

Gender Inequality Index

The Gender Inequality Index (GII), another developed by the UNDP, is based on three dimensions: reproductive health, empowerment and labor market, that is, the differences between women and men in these respects. On an international scale the highest scores are those of northern and western European countries with values close to zero. The Netherlands' Gender Inequality Index is 0.2, which is very good, while Yemen's Index would be 0.8, which is very poor. We have data for seven of the countries of Central Eurasia; they are not available for Armenia, Georgia, Turkmenistan and Uzbekistan. There are no separate data for Qinghai, Tibet and Xinjiang; the Index for China is 0.405 which is lower (better) than that for any of the Central Eurasian countries for which we have data.

Most countries in Eurasia have very similar values; Mongolia's Index is 0.523 and Georgia's is 0.597. The indexes for all the other countries are between these two.

Recent migration streams

There were no internal travel restrictions in the Soviet Union during the years after Stalin's death. One could travel to Moscow for visits, although for employment in Moscow, or other Soviet cities, one had to have *propiska* (official registration in the city of employment). The Ministry of Internal Affairs issued the *propiska* (a stamp in the individual's passport with their official address). A passport was needed for an international air ticket or hotel. Travel by Soviet citizens to strategic military areas and frontier areas (near international borders) required special permission from the Ministry of Internal Affairs. For foreigners or outsiders in early Soviet years, it was difficult to gain entry to a closed military or industrial city.

The Soviet state maintained a tight grip on internal migration. For many Soviet residents, their "dream" employment was in the Moscow region; many also had first-hand knowledge of life in the capital, had family members who traveled there for education or military purposes, or they went there as tourists at very low costs. (In the Soviet Union, travel, even over long distances, was relatively cheap.) Travel within China was also controlled. There were specific waves of migration to western areas of China from 1956 to 1964 during the rustication movements and the Great Leap Forward, and from 1990 to 2010 during the Develop the West Campaign.

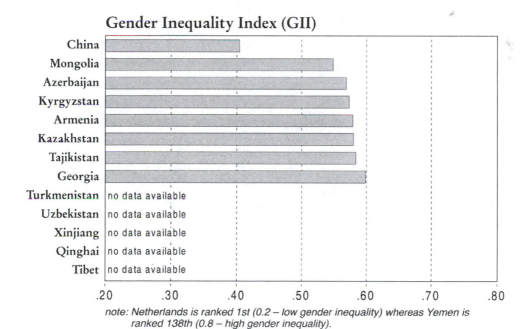

Figure 2 Gender Inequality Index (GII)

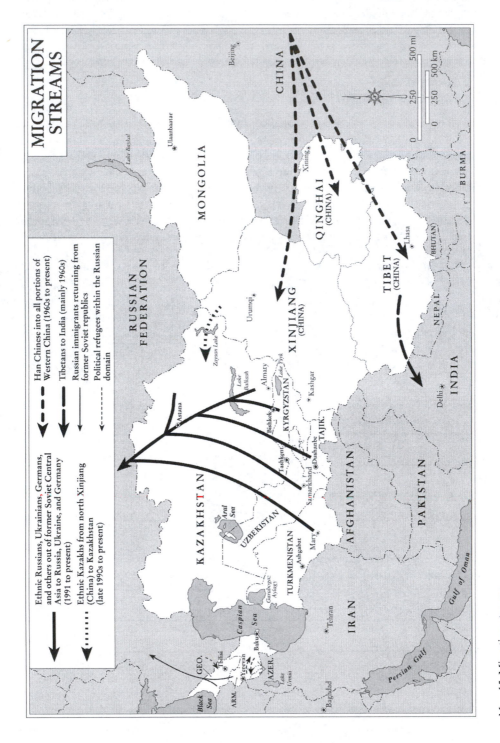

Map 15 Migration streams

The end of the Soviet Union resulted in a different set of migration streams, some of which did not exist previously. The major difference was that the movement was now interstate, for example, between Kazakhstan and Russia or between Uzbekistan and Kyrgyzstan. Previously these were movements that would have been between Soviet republics. Now crossing international borders requires some official document (a passport or an identification card), a document sometimes issued by one's new country on the world political map. Not everyone in the former Soviet Union has a passport, which is required for international travel. These individuals would have an identification card which is issued by their country of residence.

Map 15 illustrates several major patterns. First is the migration of Russians who moved from the Central Asian states, in particular, to Russia; many of these were first-time movers to Russia itself. The favored destination was Moscow, but also smaller regional cities such as Novosibirsk, Irkutsk, Barnaul and Omsk were popular. The second major migration stream was Han Chinese from central and eastern China moving into the country's western provinces. It was specific government policy to encourage Han populations in large numbers to establish residence in cities such as Urumqi, Kashgar and Lhasa, all cities with smallish Chinese populations previously, or to settle near the country's western boundaries. The Caucasus states have been a region of conflict, between Georgia and Russia in 2008 and between Armenia and Azerbaijan in 1991–94. The regional conflicts have also resulted in some cross-border migrations, with Russians, in particular, moving from Georgia into Russia.

Behind these migrations are internal changes taking place in the region's political and cultural landscapes. Russians, once in favored positions during Soviet days, now find themselves increasingly marginalized, economically and politically, in their new states. Where they were once a privileged minority, and even nearly a majority population in some areas, such as northern Kazakhstan, they now find themselves competing on often unequal terms with the titled (or ethnic majority) population for jobs in administration, universities and the commercial sector. Moving to Moscow or Novosibirsk may be a dream, a dream that will for many be unfulfilled. A direct result of many of these internal changes has been decreased proportions of Russians in major cities, including capitals, and increased proportions of non-Russians. Some Tibetans have moved into India as refugees.

In China, Han populations are moving westward into Qinghai, Tibet and Xinjiang. Some are peasants moving into agricultural areas to work in the fields, whether fields of cotton or grapes. Many are also seeking work in the cities of Lhasa, Xining, Urumqi and Kashgar. The sources of this migration are mainly Sichuan Province (the Yangtze River valley, next to Tibet), Gansu Province (next to Xinjiang and Qinghai) and Henan Province (in the Yellow River valley). This population flow follows the roads and railroads. The railroad reached Xining by 1980 and Kashgar by 1999, and in all cases it has made migration flows to Qinghai, Tibet and Xinjiang from other parts of China much easier. These are the only population flows that are moving west in China. Most flows in China trend eastward to the coast, drawn by work in factories and construction in Shanghai, Guangzhou and Beijing. Another element of migration is the rural to urban flow from Tibetan and Uyghur villages to the cities. That Tibetan or Uyghur flow then competes with Han migrants for jobs in the cities of Urumqi, Kashgar, Xining and Lhasa. External flows include Kazakhs, Uyghurs and Tibetans. Some Kazakhs have left Xinjiang for Kazakhstan, as the latter has a policy of welcoming Kazakhs from abroad. Since the 1950s there has been an outflow of Tibetans to India, joining the community in diaspora. Besides India and Nepal, there are thousands of Tibetans in the USA, Canada, Switzerland and Taiwan. Uyghurs who have moved abroad are fewer in number, traveling to Turkey, Pakistan, Afghanistan, Australia, Europe (Munich, Paris or London) or the USA (Silicon Valley, Washington, DC and New York).

Ethnic Russians: Central Asia and the Caucasus

The history of Russians in the Caucasus and Central Asia can be traced back three centuries in Central Asia and earlier in the Caucasus, to times when the Russian state sought territory to bring under its control. Russian history in these regions was not a slow and gradual process or one that was always peaceful, as there were conflicts with Mongols and other smaller groups who had to be wrestled from control by others in order to maintain vital Russian trade routes and frontier control points. It must be remembered that Russia's expansion into what today would be called Central Asia and Siberia was in areas with low population densities and few existing strong commercial ties to any external region or state. The Russian expansion in these regions was mostly to establish a Russian economic and military presence, and to prevent neighboring aggressive powers, especially China, from gaining a strong foothold.

The Russian migrations into the Caucasus were mostly to two types of areas: capital cities and industrial centers. Capital cities during the Soviet days, which were also years when rural to urban migration was emerging as a major element in the region's society, were the major focus for Soviet administrators, bureaucrats, scientists, artists and military personnel, who often resided either in exclusive residential areas if they were the party elites, or mixed with other nationals in ethnically heterogeneous neighborhoods. Russians were and are still a visible and important minority in Tbilisi, Yerevan and Baku. In the case of Central Asia, the capitals of the Soviet republics were similar in structure to those in the Caucasus. Streets and cities were laid out with Soviet planning designs. Industrial and mining centers also would have had clusters of skilled Russians.

In northern Kazakhstan the Russian pattern was different than elsewhere in Central Asia. Here Russians not only comprised large numbers of residents, but, along with other minorities, outnumbered Kazakhs in some cities. Stalin deported a great many Germans, Chechnyans, Koreans and Japanese to Central Asia, for example, to Karaganda, to work in factories. Many Russians, Ukrainians and Belorussians entered northern Kazakhstan in the 1950s and later as part of the Soviet Virgin Land Scheme under Khrushchev. They built some new towns and cities, but also there were significant numbers in the rural settlements. Russians often worked in agriculture alongside Kazakhs, but also with Germans, Ukrainians and others who came two or more centuries ago or after World War Two when Stalin deported them to this region. During the Virgin Lands Program, steppe grasslands were ploughed up and wheat was planted. Initial harvests were good; however, due to erosion and lack of fertilizer, subsequent harvests were poor. Many Russians who arrived in northern Kazakhstan as a result of these Soviet migration programs have returned to Russia, either to Moscow or to cities in southern Russia, but still very sizeable numbers remain in the cities (one-third or more of the populations of the major cities) and in the countryside. Evidence of the Russian presence is visible in languages one hears in markets and on the streets and in the bilingual signage of street names, outdoor advertising and national television. Many of the Germans have returned to Germany since the Soviet Union ended.

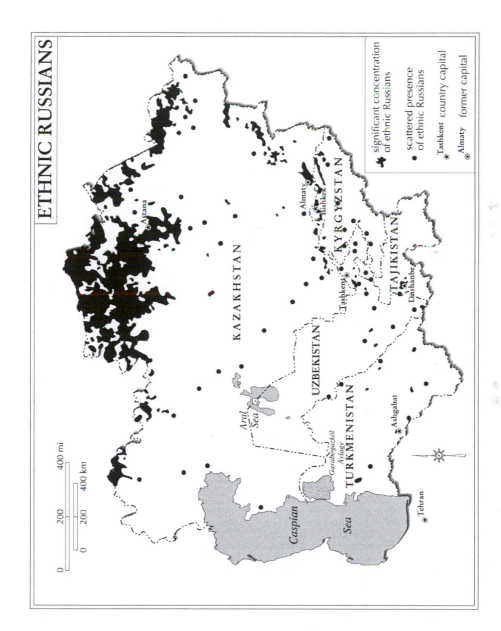

Map 16 Ethnic Russians: Central Asia

Map 17 Ethnic Russians: Caucasus

Ethnolinguistic regions

Mongolia and west China

Mongolia has 3 million people (2011 estimate). This sparsely settled land is 95 percent Mongol (of these, 86 percent are Khalkha and 14 percent are Oirat and Buryat). Almost 4 percent of the population is composed of Kazakhs who live mostly in western Mongolia. Mongols use a variation of the Cyrillic alphabet.

Minority groups are usually identified as nationalities in China. Han is the name for the ethnic Chinese group who account for 91.5 percent of the population according to the 2010 census. Among the minority groups in China, Uyghurs number approximately 11 million, Hui (whose native tongue is Chinese) around 10 million, Mongols 5–6 million, Tibetans 5 million, Kazakhs 1.5 million and Kyrgyz fewer than 200,000. Most of the Han in western China speak Mandarin as do the Hui. Many Mongols are bilingual, but a number speak only Mandarin and others only Mongol. Most Uyghurs speak their own language and some Mandarin, while a majority of Tibetans speak their own dialect (Kham, Amdo or Dbusgtsang) together with some Mandarin. Many Kazakh and Kyrgyz speak their own language as well as Uyghur and some Mandarin. Tibetans follow the Tibetan Lama variant of Buddhism, as do most Mongols. Uyghurs, Kazakh, Kyrgyz and Hui are mostly Sunni Muslims. Han are generally syncretic in their belief system, including Buddhism, Confucian and Daoist schools of thought. In China, secularism holds sway among most Han, in contrast to the case with Uyghurs and Tibetans.

In the Tibetan Autonomous Region there are 3 million people, of whom more than 94 percent are ethnic Tibetans and 4 percent are Han. Many Han live in the city of Lhasa. The south is mostly Dbusgtsang (Ü-Tsang) Tibetan while the north is mostly Kham Tibetan. Far northern Tibet is sparsely populated. Tibetan script is related to Sanskrit.

In Qinghai there are 5–6 million people, of whom 51 percent are Han, 28 percent Tibetan and 15 percent Hui. The Han are mostly in the central areas. Tibetans in the south are mostly Kham, while those in eastern Qinghai are mostly Amdo.

In Xinjiang there are 22 million people, 46 percent of whom are Uyghur, 39 percent Han, 7 percent Kazakh, 4 percent Hui, and smaller numbers (less than 1 percent each) Kyrgyz, Mongol, Xibe (Manchu), Russian and Tajik. The Uyghur live mostly in the southern part of Xinjiang in the oases around the Tarim Basin, and also in the north in Urumqi and Ili. The Han are resident mostly in the central area with some in the south (Aksu), while the Kazakh live mostly in the north, Hui mostly in the central area, and Kyrgyz and Tajik mostly in the southwest. (The Tajik in Xinjiang are Sarikoli who are distinct from Tajikistan's Tajiks; they speak a Pamir language and are Ismaili Shia). The Uyghur, Kazakh and Kyrgyz use a modified Perso-Arabic script. In the 1960s a Latinized script was used and in the 1950s a Cyrillic script was followed. Prior to the advent of the People's Republic of China, much of the writing was in a Chagatai script similar to the Arabic script used today.

Finally, in Inner Mongolia there are 25 million people. The Han population accounts for 80 percent, Mongols for 17 percent and Manchu 2 percent. Han people have been migrating to the area since the Qing Dynasty. Still, there are more Mongols in China than there are in Mongolia. The classic Mongolian script is used in Inner Mongolia today.

Central Asia

Kazakh, Kyrgyz, Uzbek, Turkmen, Uyghur and Tatar are all Turkic languages, while Tajik is an Iranian language. The people of all of these groups are predominantly Muslim.

Kazakhstan has a population of 15 million (2011 estimate). According to the 2009 census, 63 percent of the population are ethnically Kazakh, 24 percent Russian, 3 percent Uzbek, 2 percent Ukrainian, 1.5 percent Uyghur, 1 percent Tatar and 1 percent German. While 64 percent of the population uses Kazakh as the lingua franca, 95 percent of the population uses Russian. The religious mix is Muslim 47 percent, Russian Orthodox 44 percent and 2 percent Protestant. Kazakh is a Turkic language which uses a Cyrillic alphabet. There are also 1.5 million Kazakhs in Xinjiang, China and almost 1 million in Uzbekistan. Russians, Ukrainians and Germans (the few that remain) are resident mostly in north Kazakhstan and Almaty, while Uzbeks, Uyghurs and Tatars live mostly in the south.

Kyrgyzstan has a population of 5.5 million (2011 estimate). According to the 1999 census, 65 percent of the population are ethnically Kyrgyz, 14 percent are Uzbek, 12 percent Russian, 1 percent Hui (Dungan), 1 percent Ukrainian, 1 percent Uyghur and 6 percent other. The religious mix is 75 percent Muslim and 20 percent Russian Orthodox. Kyrgyz is a Turkic language which also uses the Cyrillic alphabet. There are 3.8 million Kyrgyz in Kyrgyzstan, 250,000 Kyrgyz in Uzbekistan and 145,000 Kyrgyz in Xinjiang, China. Also there are 760,000 Uzbeks in Kyrgyzstan, most living in the Fergana Valley, while the resident Russians live mostly in the northern part of the country.

Tajikistan has a population of 7.6 million (2011 estimate), of which 80 percent are Tajik, 15 percent Uzbek, 1 percent Russian and 1 percent Kyrgyz. Tajik is an Iranian language (like Farsi or Persian) and is currently written with a Cyrillic alphabet, although the country may move to a Perso-Arabic script. The religious mix is 85 percent Sunni Muslim and

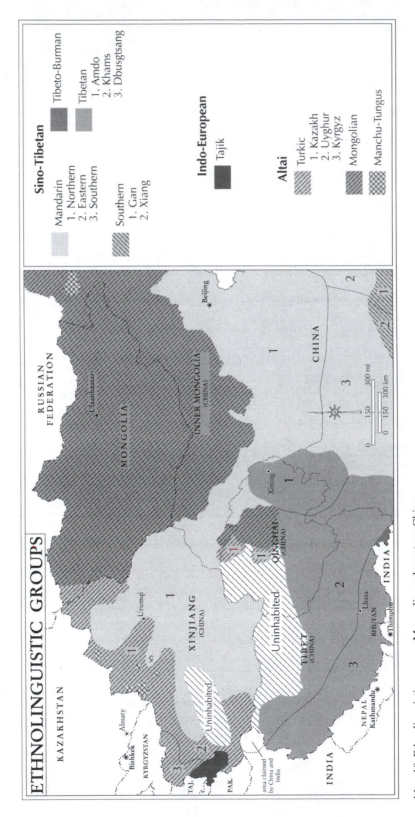

Map 18 Ethnolinguistic groups: Mongolia and western China

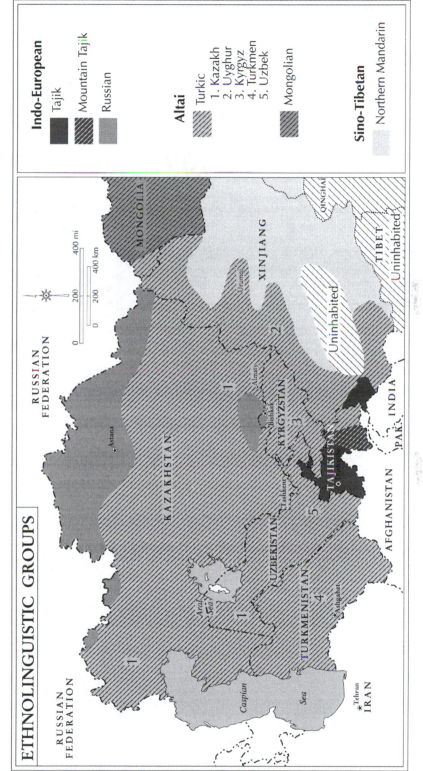

ETHNOLINGUISTIC GROUPS

Indo-European

Tajik

Mountain Tajik

Russian

Altai

Turkic
1. Kazakh
2. Uyghur
3. Kyrgyz
4. Turkmen
5. Uzbek

Mongolian

Sino-Tibetan

Northern Mandarin

RUSSIAN FEDERATION

RUSSIAN FEDERATION

MONGOLIA

KAZAKHSTAN

Astana

1

1

Aral Sea

Caspian

Sea

Tehran
IRAN

TURKMENISTAN

Ashgabat

4

UZBEKISTAN

Tashkent

5

KYRGYZSTAN

Bishkek

3

Almaty

1

XINJIANG

Urumqi

2

Uninhabited

QINGHAI

TIBET
Uninhabited

TAJIKISTAN

AFGHANISTAN

PAK.

INDIA

0   200   400 km

0   200   400 mi

Map 19 Ethnolinguistic groups: Central Asia

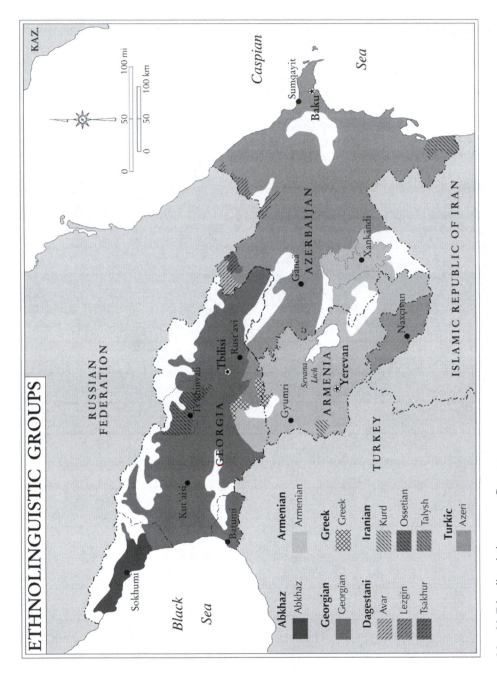

Map 20 Ethnolinguistic groups: Caucasus

5 percent Shia Muslim. The Mountain Tajik are mostly Ismail Shia and speak eastern Iranian languages such as Wakhi and Shugni. Otherwise Tajik and Russian are the most common languages. The Uzbeks live mostly in the west and Kyrgyz in the east. There are 6 million Tajiks in Tajikistan, 8–11 million in Afghanistan, 1.4 million in Uzbekistan and 1.2 million in Pakistan.

Turkmenistan has a population of 5 million (2011 estimate). According to 2003 estimates, 85 percent of the population are Turkmen, 5 percent Uzbek and 4 percent Russian. Turkmen is a Turkic language and the country is shifting from a Cyrillic to a Latin script. The religious mix is 89 percent Muslim and 9 percent Russian Orthodox. Turkmen (72 percent) and Russian (12 percent) are the most common languages. The country's Uzbeks live mostly in the north. There are 5.5 million Turkmen in Turkmenistan, 1.3 million in Iran and 1 million in Afghanistan.

Uzbekistan has a population of 28 million (2011 estimate). According to 1996 estimates, 80 percent of the population are Uzbek, 5 percent Russian, 3 percent Kazakh, 3 percent Karakalpak and 1.5 percent Tatar. The religious mix is 88 percent Sunni and 9 percent Russian Orthodox. Uzbek is a Turkic language and the country is moving from a Cyrillic to a Latin script. There are 22–23 million Uzbeks in Uzbekistan and there are also 2–3 million in Afghanistan, 1 million in Tajikistan, 760,000 in Kyrgyzstan, 470,000 in Kazakhstan and 250,000 in Turkmenistan. The country's Kazakhs mostly reside in the north, Karakalpaks in the west and Tatars in the cities. In southern Uzbekistan, many people also have a Tajik background but speak Uzbek. Uzbek and Russian are the most common languages.

Caucasus

Armenia has a population of 3 million (2011 estimate). According to the 2001 census, 98 percent of the population are ethnically Armenian, 1.3 percent are Yezdi (Kurd) and 0.5 percent Russian. Many people speak both Armenian and Russian. Most ethnic Armenians follow the Armenian Apostolic Church, with smaller numbers of Sunni Islam or Russian Orthodox. The Armenian alphabet was devised in the fifth century and is still used to write the language.

Azerbaijan has a population of 8.3 million (2011 estimate). According to the latest census (1999), 91 percent are Azeri, 2 percent are Dagestani, 2 percent Russian and 1 percent Armenian. (Most of the Armenians live in the disputed Nagorno-Karabakh region.) The Azeri and Dagestani are mostly Sunni Muslim, Russians are Russian Orthodox and Armenians are Armenian Orthodox. Azeri is a Turkic language and the country is moving from a Cyrillic to a Latin script. Many Azeris speak both Azeri and Russian. There are also 12 million Azeris in Iran who use a Perso-Arabic alphabet.

Georgia has a population of 4.5 million (2011 estimate). According to the 2002 census, 84 percent of the population are ethnically Georgian, 6 percent Azeri, 6 percent Armenian, 2 percent Russian and 2 percent other. Georgian is a South Caucasus (Kartvelian) language and uses its own alphabet. There are about 100,000 Abkhazians, most living in Abkhazia, who speak a Caucasus language; Abkhaz, is their official language. There are also about 85,000 Ossetians, most of whom reside in South Ossetia. (Some 500,000 Ossetians live in North Ossetia in Russia). Ossetian is an Iranian language. Georgians and Russians follow Orthodox Christianity, Azeris follow Islam, while Armenians follow the Armenian Apostolic Church.

Urban population

There are some sharp differences between countries in this region. The areas where the highest percentages of the population live in cities are Armenia (64 percent), Kazakhstan (58 percent), Georgia and Mongolia (57 percent each). The lowest percentages are in the three Chinese provinces (Xinjiang and Qinghai 35 percent each and Tibet 25 percent) as well as Uzbekistan (37 percent), Kyrgyzstan (36 percent) and Tajikistan (only 26 percent). In all Central Eurasian countries, except Kazakhstan (where former capital Almaty has 1.4 million and current capital Astana only 725,000), the capital city has a population several times the size of the second ranking city. In Mongolia, for example, Ulaanbaatar has a population of 949,000 while Erdenet has only 90,000. This dominance of the capital city is also reflected in Tbilisi, Yerevan and Baku which have 45 percent, 60 percent and 45 percent respectively of their countries urban populations. The capitals are not only the major administrative and political centers, but also the cities with most offices of major transnational corporations, museums, galleries, zoos, parks, sports arenas and entertainment centers. In the west China regions, Urumqi, Xining and Lhasa are the major urban centers in provinces which still have more rural than urban residents.

The largest city in Central Asia is Tashkent (2.2 million), an old city on the Silk Road that has held economic and political prominence in the region for centuries. In many ways this historic city epitomizes the reasons for growth, given that it is the country's capital, it is home to major industrial economies, it is close to the prosperous Fergana Valley for agriculture, and boasts some of Central Eurasia's major universities, theaters, operas and athletic teams.

Aside from the state capitals there are other major urban centers in the region that are important. First, one should not omit Astana, Kazakhstan's new capital in the north-central part of the country. This basically new city (it was only a small urban settlement before the president decided to locate the capital here in the mid-1990s) has all the appearances of a postmodern city created in a desert environment. It was originally called Tselinograd, built during the Virgin Land years; later its name was changed to Akmola and then to Astana in the mid-1990s. Astana's present population of 700,000 plus residents and visitors can observe its stunning picturesque Disneyfied buildings in a living environment associated with southern Siberia: long and very cold winters and extremely hot and dry summers. Kazakhstan's other major cities are primarily industrial centers, old cities such as Karaganda or growing cities, such as Atyrau and Aktau on the Caspian Sea, which thrive because of very productive oil and gas economies. Elsewhere around Kazakhstan's periphery one finds small industrial and administrative cities.

In Mongolia, Ulaanbaatar is the primary center with a population ten times the second largest city of Erdenet. Originally in the 1600s the capital was named Urga, but by 1925, its name was changed to Ulaan (red) baatar (hero) reflecting the new community politics of the country.

In China, Urumqi (Ürümchi, Wulumuqi) is, with a population of 2.3 million, just slightly larger than Tashkent and therefore able to claim the title of the most populous city in Central Eurasia. This city, originally called Dihua in the 1700s, was, in 1954, renamed Urumqi which means "beautiful pastures" in Junggar Mongol. Urumqi is an important economic center in western China. In Qinghai, Xining has a population of 1 million. The city was first called Xining in the twelfth century; "xi" means west and "ning" means pacify in Chinese. In the Tibet Autonomous Region, Lhasa, means "place of the gods" in Tibetan, has a population of some 375,000; it is an old cultural center dating back to the ninth century.

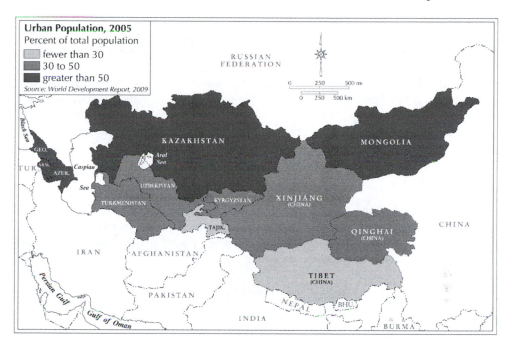

Map 21 Urban population, 2005

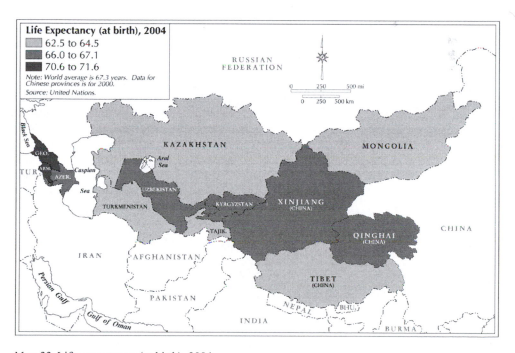

Map 22 Life expectancy (at birth), 2004

Life expectancy

Data on life expectancy are not collected annually by most countries, thus we have to rely on what is available to illustrate the present situation. The United Nations data used for Map 22 are from 2004, which is the latest set available for the region and for making cross-country comparisons. It would be desirable to have finer grained geographic data when looking at life expectancy, that is, data on some minor administrative units, as one associates with demographic data analysis in Europe and North America. In the absence of such urban and rural data, however, we have to rely on national scale data. Distinct variations do show up between the wealthier and poorer states or administered regions. Unsurprisingly, we learn that residents in two of the three (not Azerbaijan) Caucasus states have rates exceeding 70 years. At the other end of the continuum we find a mix of states, some with high incomes that have among the lowest rates, less than 65 years. This group of states includes Mongolia, Kazakhstan, Tajikistan and Turkmenistan. While China overall has a life expectancy of 71, western China is lower, with Tibet at 64, Qinghai at 66 and Xinjiang at 67. Life expectancy in most countries has a gender difference, with women having higher rates than men.

If one compared Central Eurasia with countries in Europe, one would discover that the life expectancy rates in Europe, for women and men, exceed the rates in this region. However, the Central Asian rates are likely to be higher than those for China overall and for South Asian countries.

5 Environment

Climate

The major distinguishing feature of Central Eurasia's climate is the dominance of dry climates and subsequently low amounts of rainfall. The dry climate regions, shown as BWk (mid-latitude desert) and BSk (mid-latitude steppe), are extensions of the vast areas of aridity that stretch across nearly one-third of Africa and into southwest Asia. Deserts are regions of little or no vegetation; steppes are grasslands or pasture areas suitable for raising wheat and some livestock, especially sheep and goats. Areas of perpetual aridity, such as the extensive areas that stretch from Turkmenistan into northwest China and Mongolia, are dominated by high pressure cells and belts for much of the year. The subtropical high pressure cell is the dominant pressure system during the summer; it basically prevents any regular rainfall from occurring. In addition the Himalayan mountain system effectively blocks rainfall that might come from monsoon South Asia. The windward side receives orographic rain; Central Asia is on the leeward side and receives little or none. Little moisture comes from the Mediterranean. In short, Central Asia has a continental climate (very hot in summer; very cold – the Siberian high – in winter) and is distant from any major moisture sources. Any low pressure cells in this mid-latitude westerly wind belt would have central European or Mediterranean sources and would lose moisture as they moved inland into continental Central Eurasia. The unpredictability of sustained rainfall regimes makes it difficult to raise crops that require significant amounts of moisture.

Temperature extremes are associated with continentality, that is, the heating and cooling of this large land mass, which has some of the coldest regions on the planet. These are identified with the Dwc or Subarctic label. Summer temperatures in central Kazakhstan can reach 120 °F (49 °C). Summers in northern Kazakhstan come late, perhaps in mid-May or even June, and seldom last more than several months. Winters in the northern part of Central Eurasia are cold to very cold, with January temperatures being –49 °F (–45 °C) or colder. It is probably best to consider northern Kazakhstan and Mongolia as extensions of southern Siberia's climate. In these high latitudes, where the summers are short and, consequently, the winters are long, crop agriculture is limited to grains that can mature in a short growing season. Northern Kazakhstan is considered part of the region's "bread basket," whereas fresh fruits and vegetables are raised in southern and warmer climates which serve urban markets throughout Central Eurasia.

Aside from the huge swath of arid land that dominates the region's climate, there are two other distinctive climate regions. One is the large section of southwest China, especially Tibet and Qinghai, which has a highland climate. The Himalayan mountain system, which has some of the highest peaks in the world, effectively blocks monsoon rains from South Asia from entering western China and Central Asia. The area of the highland climates is

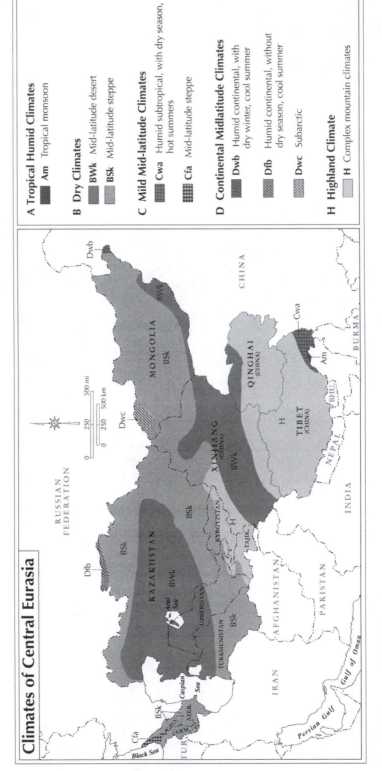

Map 23 Climates of Central Eurasia

also a region of sparse population, very few cities and few extensive areas of productive agriculture. Being too cold, having a very short growing season and an irregular terrain precludes any large-scale crop agriculture. What crops are raised are found in the river valleys where level land and good soils exist. Livestock herding is also associated with many of the pastoral economies of highland Central Eurasia.

A small but important climate region for Central Eurasia exists in the Caucasus, especially in Georgia. The three states in this region are in a mid-latitude region that has more rainfall, milder temperatures and a longer growing season than elsewhere in arid or highland Central Eurasia. Seasonal vegetables and fruits can be grown here that cannot be produced elsewhere in the region. In many ways, the Caucasus states are like the irrigated croplands of Central Eurasia in that they provide many of the fresh summer products for capital cities and regional administrative centers.

Climographs

Climographs provide a graphic presentation of monthly average temperatures and rates of precipitation. They illustrate the seasonal variations in temperature and precipitation. Most of the cities in the Central Eurasia region are in the BSk (mid-latitude steppe) climate. Tbilisi has a Cfa Humid subtropical climate. Ulaanbaatar approaches a subarctic climate (Dwc). Ashgabat and Urumqi approach an arid climate (BWk).

Mongolia and west China

Ulaanbaatar, Mongolia (BSk climate) lies in the foothills of the Bogd Khan Uul Mountains. This city is the coldest capital in the world, averaging 28 °F (–2 °C), and is quite dry, receiving on average 9 in (229 mm) of precipitation per year. The city very nearly approaches subarctic weather, including permafrost conditions.

Xining, Qinghai, China (BSk climate) is located on the eastern edge of the Tibetan Plateau. Summers are cool and winters are very cold. The precipitation averages 24 in (609 mm) per year with a summer maximum.

Lhasa, Tibet, China (BSk climate) lies in the greater Yarlung River valley in the Tibetan Plateau at an elevation of 1,197 ft (3,650 m). Summers are cool and winters are cold, but the city is very sunny. Precipitation is limited, averaging 17 in (431 mm) per year, with a summer maximum.

Urumqi, Xinjiang, China (BSk climate) lies in a cleft of the Tian Shan range and receives its water from the glaciers in the mountains. The city is the farthest large city from any ocean. Continentality ensures cold winters and hot summers. Annual precipitation averages 10 in (254 mm) (meaning it is almost desert) with a spring maximum.

Central Asia

Astana, Kazakhstan (BSk climate) lies in the steppe lands close to Siberia, so winters are very cold. The capital has a summer maximum of precipitation, averaging only 13 in (330 mm) per year.

Almaty (BSk climate), the former capital of Kazakhstan, lies north of the Alatau Mountains, a branch of the Tian Shan. The mountains generate orographic precipitation, so the city has a more substantial spring rainfall, although the summer is drier. The annual average is 26 in (660 mm). The city is warmer than Astana.

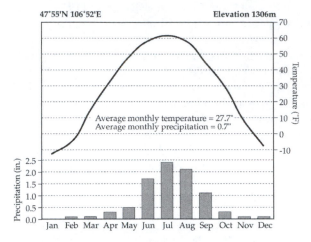

Figure 3a Climograph for Ulaanbaatar, Mongolia

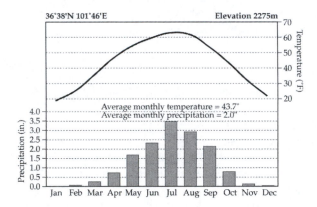

Figure 3b Climograph for Xining, Qinghai

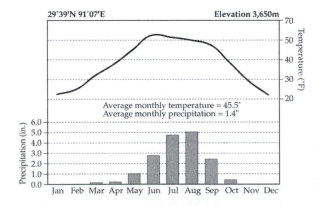

Figure 3c Climograph for Lhasa, Tibet

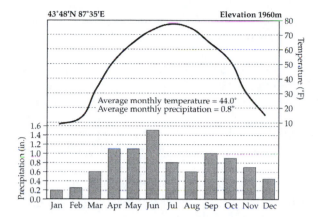

Figure 3d Climograph for Urumqi, Xinjiang

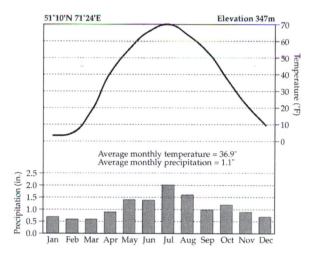

Figure 4a Climograph for Astana, Kazakhstan

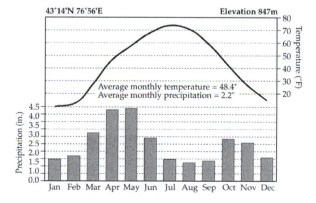

Figure 4b Climograph for Almaty, Kazakhstan

Bishkek, Kyrgyzstan (BSk climate) lies in a valley of the Alatau (Ala Too range). The city has a spring maximum of precipitation, with an annual average of 18 in (457 mm). Climate patterns are similar to those of Almaty. Mountains to the south protect the city from winter weather.

Dushanbe, Tajikistan (BSk climate) lies in a valley of the Altay mountain range. The city is farther south and protected by the mountains from the Siberian air masses and so is warmer than Almaty and Bishkek. Summers are very dry and spring sees the most precipitation, the annual average being 22 in (558 mm).

Ashgabat, Turkmenistan (BSk climate) lies north of the Kopet Dag range and south of the Garagum (Black Desert). The climate is quite dry, averaging 10 in (254 mm) per year, and is almost desert.

Tashkent, Uzbekistan (BSk climate) lies in a plain to the west of the Tian Shan, which separates the city from the Fergana Valley. The city has a hot and dry summer and a milder spring. The yearly average precipitation is 16 in (406 mm).

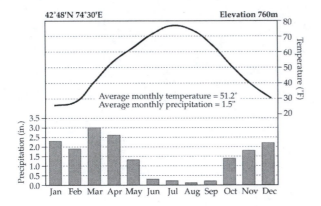

Figure 4c Climograph for Bishkek, Kyrgyzstan

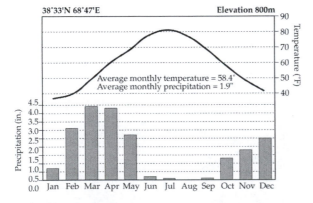

Figure 5a Climograph for Dushanbe, Tajikistan

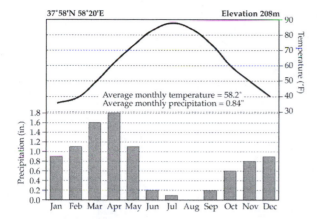

Figure 5b Climograph for Ashgabat, Turkmenistan

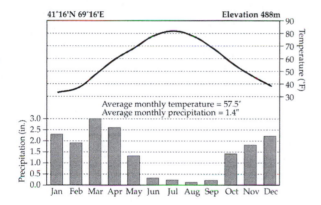

Figure 5c Climograph for Tashkent, Uzbekistan

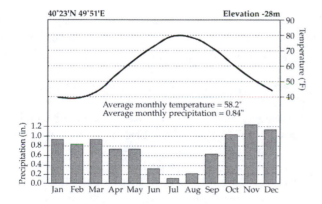

Figure 6a Climograph for Baku, Azerbaijan

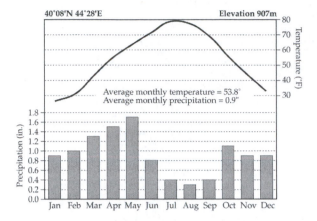

Figure 6b Climograph for Yerevan, Armenia

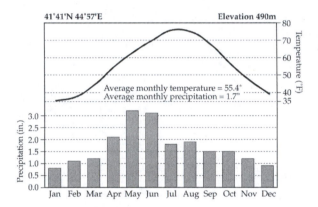

Figure 6c Climograph for Tbilisi, Georgia

Caucasus

Yerevan, Armenia (BSk climate) lies in the heart of the Armenian highland in the Ararat Valley. The city is semiarid, receiving an average of 11 in (27.5 cm) of precipitation per year with a spring maximum. Winters are mild and snowy; summers are hot and somewhat dry.

Baku, Azerbaijan (BSk Climate) is located on the west coast of the Caspian Sea. The city receives an average of 10 in (254 mm) of precipitation per year and is classified as semiarid, that is, almost a desert. The summers are dry and hot. Most of the precipitation occurs during the cooler winter. The Caspian Sea ameliorates the heat during the summer and keeps the winters mild.

Tbilisi, Georgia (Cfa climate) has a moderate humid subtropical climate. The city is in the foothills of the Caucasus Mountains about 100 miles (161 km) from the Black Sea. The city receives an average of 20 in (50 cm) of precipitation per year; the mountains block the dry Central Asian air masses. Summers are warm and winters are mild.

Precipitation

The single dominant feature of the precipitation map is the extensive area with less than 10 in (25 cm) of rain per year. All of Uzbekistan falls into this rainfall category as well as three-quarters of Kazakhstan, Turkmenistan and Mongolia. Approximately half of Xinjiang and Tibet are in this lowest precipitation category. The second lowest precipitation category includes areas receiving 10–19 inches (25–47.5 cm) per year, which is enough, if the rains come and if they come at the right time, for grain areas in northern Kazakhstan and livestock economies in eastern Kazakhstan, Mongolia, Kyrgyzstan and Tajikistan. The chief reasons why Central Asia receives so little precipitation, as noted above, are because as an area with continental climates it is dominated by very strong high pressure cells in the summer (subtropical highs) and winter (Siberian highs) and because the region is a long distance from potential sources of much moisture. It is deep within the Eurasian subcontinent and any precipitation will have its origins in low pressure systems entering from Central Europe or the Mediterranean Sea and from South Asia during monsoon seasons. Rainfall amounts drop off sharply as one moves eastward from the Caucasus states, which receive an ample amount of precipitation for a productive crop/livestock economy.

Aside from the Caucasus states, the only other area with high precipitation is the Himalayas and adjacent parts of the Tibetan Plateau. The source of rainfall here is the on-shore spring and summer monsoons that are so vital for Indian agricultural, industrial and residential use. Some of these storms on the windward side of the Himalayas are powerful enough to ascend the Himalaya and the plateau and bring good amounts of rainfall. But these are both regions not conducive to any extensive or intensive agriculture because of extremely rugged terrain in these high altitudes.

Aside from the productive agricultural areas in the mountains, valleys and coastlines of the Caucasus, the largest area of cropland agriculture is in northern Kazakhstan, or the Virgin Lands, an area of extensive frontier agriculture developed by the Soviets during the 1960s. The relatively flat terrain with productive *chernozem* (black earth) soils and moderate amounts of rainfall were ideal for large-scale (extensive in size) or state farms. Hugh grain farms are still the dominant rural and agricultural economy in much of this region today. However, high yielding harvests each year are unlikely, again because of the moisture sources from Central and Eastern European regions to the west.

Finally, in many of the other extensive areas receiving less than 20 in (508 mm) per year, one would find pastoral economies, usually sheep and horses, and also cattle, the type of economies one would associate with highland areas where the soils are not conducive to extensive crop agriculture. Transhumance, or the movement of livestock (sheep and horses) to highland areas of good pastures during the summer, is still practiced in mountainous areas of Central Asia.

Biomes

A biome is a large natural area that contains distinctive flora and fauna. The planet has many different biomes, just like climate and landform regions. Comparable regions to consider alongside biomes are climate regions, since climates are a major determinant, along with soils, of dominant vegetation.

In Central Asia a dozen different biome types exist. By far the largest areas, not unexpectedly, are in Desert and Semidesert; these are also the largest climate regions, stretching from the Caspian Sea into southern Mongolia and western China. The difference

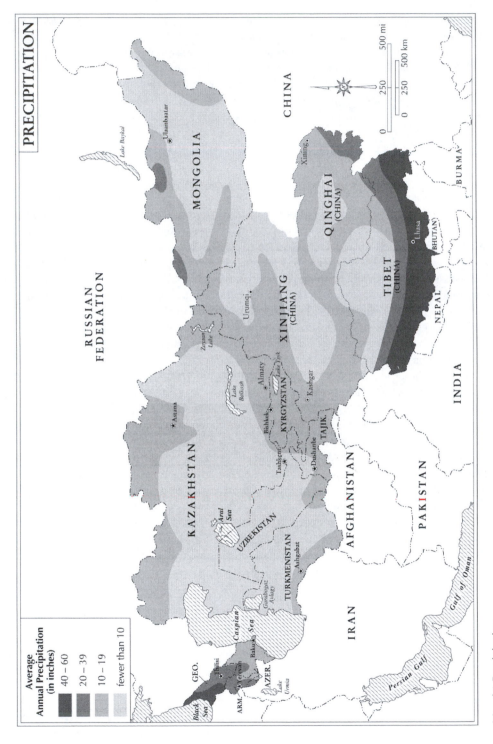

PRECIPITATION

Average Annual Precipitation (in inches)
- 40 – 60
- 20 – 39
- 10 – 19
- fewer than 10

RUSSIAN FEDERATION

MONGOLIA

Ulaanbaatar

Lake Baykal

CHINA

XINJIANG (CHINA)

Urumqi

QINGHAI (CHINA)

Xining

TIBET (CHINA)

Lhasa

NEPAL

BHUTAN

BURMA

INDIA

PAKISTAN

AFGHANISTAN

KAZAKHSTAN

Astana

Lake Balkash

Zaysan Lake

Almaty

Bishkek

KYRGYZSTAN

Lake Issyk

Kashgar

Tashkent

TAJIK.

Dushanbe

UZBEKISTAN

Aral Sea

TURKMENISTAN

Ashgabat

Garabogaz Aylagy

Caspian Sea

IRAN

Persian Gulf

Gulf of Oman

GEO.

Tbilisi

ARM.

Yerevan

AZER.

Baku

Lake Urmia

Black Sea

500 mi

500 km

0   250

0   250

Map 24 Precipitation

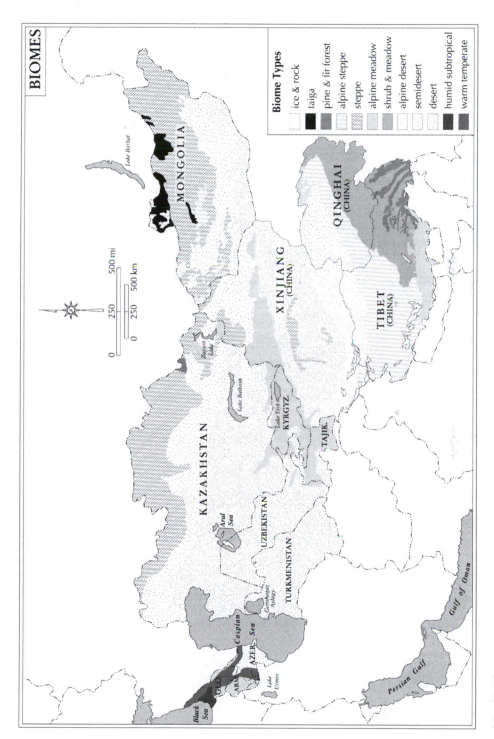

Map 25 Biomes

between these two biomes is the vegetation cover; the Desert will have limited vegetation and often only a rock or sometimes dune surface, whereas the Semidesert will be a steppe or short grasslands (no trees except along river banks and in more moist areas). These areas are by and large sparsely inhabited because it is difficult to sustain any extensive crop agriculture, except in irrigated river valleys, oases and higher mid-latitude elevations.

In the northern part of Central Eurasia, for example, in northern Mongolia, there is more moisture. Here one finds taiga or a vegetation landscape of pine and other fir trees. This region is the southern extension of the huge Siberian coniferous forest that dominates much of the eastern two-thirds of Russia.

Alpine forests are associated with major mountain chains, not only the Himalayan system, but also the Tian Shan and other ranges in southeast Kazakhstan, Kyrgyzstan and most of Tajikistan. The Himalayan mountain system comprises several different biomes, including alpine meadows, shrublands and alpine desert.

The diversity of biomes in the region extends to the Caucasus. While not nearly as extensive as the Himalayan system or steppes, it is distinctive because it represents one of the very few areas of Central Eurasia that has a distinctly different flora and faunal mix in a small area. It is labeled Human Subtropical, the same biome one finds in the southeast USA. The warm and humid summers and mild winters stand in sharp contrast to the dominant Desert and Semidesert biomes in much of the region.

Landforms

The Central Asian region is far from having a uniform topography. What distinguishes this region are the extensive areas of some of its major features. Three major and three minor regions stand out from the accompanying map. The first major landform region is the Tibetan Plateau which includes all of Tibet and half of Qinghai Province. The southern part of the plateau borders the Himalayan system; average elevation in the plateau is more than 14,800 ft or 4,500 m. Peaks in the Himalaya system range from Mt Kailash at 21,778 ft or 6,638 m and Mt K2 (Khogir) at 28,251 ft or 8,611 m to Mt Everest at 29,035 ft or 8,848 m.

The second extensive area includes the huge basins in Xinjiang and Mongolia; on landform maps these are identified as the Taklamakan Desert (in Xinjiang) and the Gobi Desert (much of Mongolia). These areas, as other maps in this atlas illustrate, are sparsely populated and have pastoral livelihoods or, in a few places, oasis agriculture.

The third distinctive landform region is the extensive desert and steppe regions that cover most of Turkmenistan and Uzbekistan and much of central and western Kazakhstan. Names given to specific regions are the Kyzyl Kum (in Uzbekistan), Garagum (Turkmenistan) and Kyrgyz Steppe (much of Kazakhstan). Where there is somewhat more moisture, as in the steppes, the soils and surface conditions permit extensive grain (wheat) agriculture; where rain comes very irregularly, pastoral (sheep, goats and horses) economies exist, and where there is almost no rain, there is little or no permanent agriculture or settlement. The desert areas are extremely dry, some places not receiving any rain during a year, and basically absent of any vegetation.

The first minor landform region is the Caucasus, a moderately high area (10,000–12,000 ft, 3,050–3,660 m elevation in places) between the Caspian and the Black Sea. This formidable landform region separates Russia from Georgia and Azerbaijan. As is pointed out elsewhere in this atlas, this boundary region has been the site of historical and contemporary conflicts between the Soviet Union or Russia and neighboring countries to the south. In the Caucasus

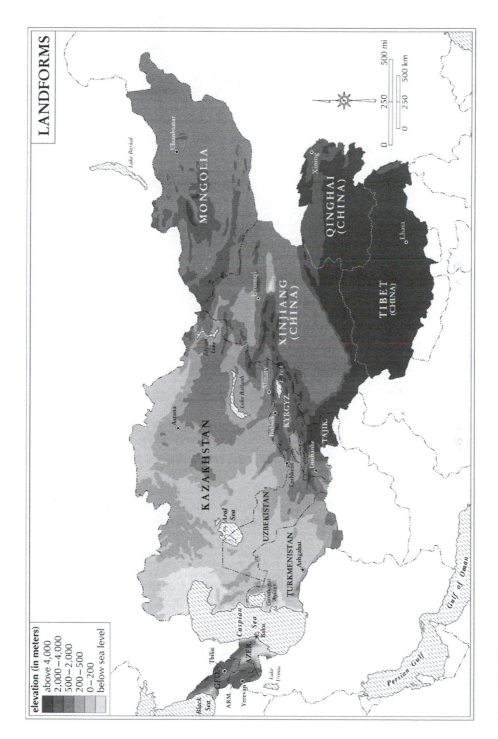

LANDFORMS

elevation (in meters)
- above 4,000
- 2,000 – 4,000
- 500 – 2,000
- 200 – 500
- 0 – 200
- below sea level

Black Sea

Tbilisi

GEO.

ARM.

Yerevan

AZER.

Baku

Lake Urmia

Caspian Sea

Persian Gulf

Gulf of Oman

TURKMENISTAN

Ashgabat

Garabogaz Aylagy

Aral Sea

UZBEKISTAN

Tashkent

KAZAKHSTAN

Astana

Lake Balkash

Almaty

Bishkek

KYRGYZ

Dushanbe

TAJIK.

Urumqi

Zaysan Lake

XINJIANG (CHINA)

MONGOLIA

Ulaanbaatar

Lake Baikal

QINGHAI (CHINA)

Xining

TIBET (CHINA)

Lhasa

0   250   500 mi

0   250   500 km

Map 26 Landforms

one finds some of the greatest diversity of languages and ethnicity on the planet. Its subtropical location has made it one of the most productive agricultural areas of the former Soviet Union.

The second minor region is the area in and around the Caspian Sea. This region is known historically and most recently for its rich oil and gas fields, its thriving petrochemical industrial base and its strong banking economy. Landform-wise, there are areas in the eastern and northeastern part of Caspian that are below sea level. The Caspian itself is 90 ft (27.5 m) below sea level. The Aral Sea, not far away, is only 135 ft (41 m) above sea level.

The third minor and distinctive landform region is the Pamirs, which are in southeastern Tajikistan. Physical geographers, geomorphologists and geologists often refer to the Pamir Knot when discussing mountainous regions in Asia. Three branches emerge from the Pamirs: one is associated with the Himalayan system, another is the Tian Shan (Tenghri Tagh) which extends into eastern Kyrgyzstan, southeastern and eastern Kazakhstan and into western China, and the third cuts westward across northern Afghanistan and Iran.

Detailed landform maps would identify many more minor regions, including mountain ranges, deserts, depressions and valleys.

Water features

From what was described above about climate regions, that is, distinctive temperature and precipitation characteristics, there are four major features about water in this region, which is roughly the size of South America. First is that Central Eurasia for all intents and purposes is a landlocked region, that is, it has no direct access to any of the world's oceans or major regional water bodies. It might be argued that, by virtue of Georgia bordering the Black Sea, Central Eurasia is not landlocked. We prefer to consider this entire territory as landlocked. What this statement implies is that, for any of the Central Eurasian states and western Chinese provinces to have access to a large water body, such as an ocean, it must "go through" one or two or three or more states to enter an ocean or a large sea. Some of the states are double and triple landlocked.

Second, proximity to water is a very important variable in explaining population distribution and economic activity. Most of the large cities (and there are exceptions) are located along major rivers or the headwaters of major rivers. Examples are the string of cities along the Irtysh River in northern Kazakhstan and those along minor rivers in southeastern Kazakhstan and northern Kyrgyzstan and the capitals in Turkmenistan, Tajikistan and Mongolia.

Third, there are many small rivers where there is interior drainage, that is, the rivers flow into interior lakes rather than to larger rivers which may flow out of the region. Some of these, such as the Syr Darya in Kazakhstan and the Amu Darya in Uzbekistan, are very important in irrigated cotton economies and also extensive fruit and vegetable areas. One can also discover these interior draining situations in Tajikistan, eastern Kazakhstan, Mongolia and western China.

Fourth, the politics or geopolitics of water will continue to play a role in water availability and distribution. The politics include upstream and downstream interstate politics. Several examples illustrate this telling point. Kyrgyzstan, a small landlocked state the size of Switzerland, is one of the poorest in the region, but has immense hydropower potential. Countries downstream, Uzbekistan and Tajikistan, would like to have more of the waters

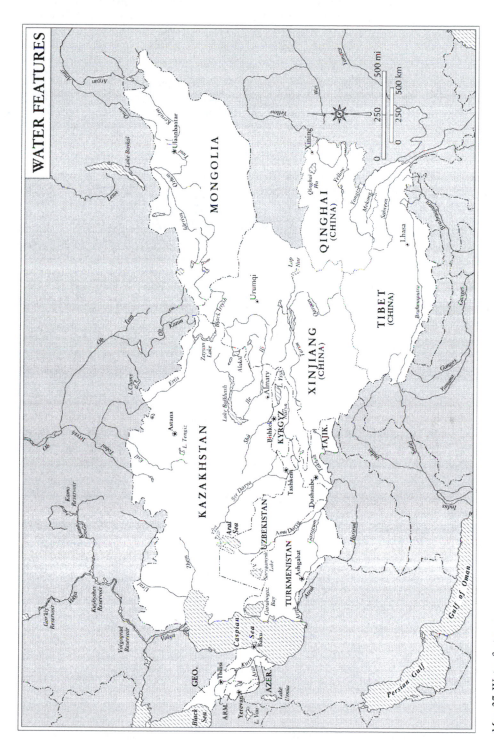

Map 27 Water features

available for agricultural and industrial purposes. Often countries outside Central Asia are playing the "water game" with Central Asian states. China is often cited as but one example of a country that could "cut off" or reduce water supplies to Irtysh (Ertis) river cities in northern Kazakhstan, northwest China or those rivers serving cities in southern Eurasia.

There is little doubt but that the local, regional and extraregional politics of water will continue to be a major development issue in rural and urban Central Eurasia. The demands for water that exist for agricultural needs will only be heightened with growing populations in urban areas, including urban population explosions (the case for Astana, which has no major river running through it) and high density rural populations in the Fergana Valley and elsewhere.

The Yellow, Yangtze, Mekong, Salween, Brahmaputra and Indus all have their headwaters in the Tibetan Qinghai plateau. Northern China has a great demand for water. The state has been studying the possibility of moving water from the Yangtze River in the south to the Yellow River in the north, a south to north water transfer project. Engineering projects have already been started in the eastern part of the country. The state is also studying the feasibility of bringing water from the Mekong and Salween to the Yellow River. Environmental problems would result. Similarly the state is investigating damming the Brahmaputra for hydroelectric projects in Tibet. In this case downstream users in India and Bangladesh would be negatively affected. Southern Xinjiang relies on the Tarim River, on which the state has many irrigation projects. Now the Tarim no longer reaches Lop Nur. China also utilizes the Ili and Irtysh (Ertis) rivers for irrigation. Overutilization of the Ili River will mean further desiccation of Lake Balkash in Kazakhstan.

Access to improved water

This issue might be considered a good variable by which to measure quality of life, in that clean and potable drinking water is usually high on the list of a country's priorities for human development. Having access to improved drinking water usually means that water is obtained from a municipal water system, not from a standpipe or community well.

The availability of water from a municipal system is probably best correlated with the percentage of the population living in cities. That is, the higher the percentage of the population living in cities, the higher the percentage having access to improved water sources. This relationship applies to the three Caucasus states and also Kazakhstan, all of which have more than half of their residents living in cities. Elsewhere, as another map in this atlas illustrates, there are fewer than 30 percent of the population living in cities in Tibet and Tajikistan and 30–50 percent in the rest of the countries and Chinese provinces.

The situation in cities is one where water and electricity are available, except for newly developed residential areas for informal housing where both running water and electricity may not exist. In most large cities, which are the sites of major political, economic and administrative activities, there are water systems that connect both the older parts of the cities and also suburbs, including areas on the peripheries where there are vast complexes of high density housing built during socialist years.

In countries where perhaps only 30 or 40 percent of the population lives in cities, the water picture is likely to be dramatically different. The capital city and major industrial and commercial cities are likely to have a good water supply system. In rural areas and small towns, there may be no city water system. Rather, people obtain water from a stand-

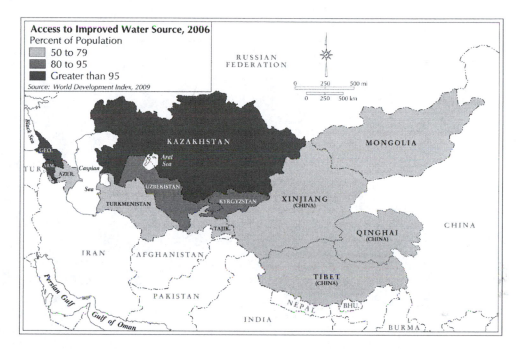

Map 28 Access to improved water, 2006

pipe in their community. The same source is used for gathering water for drinking as for cleaning pots and pans, preparing food and water for bathing. Outside toilets are commonplace, not indoor plumbing as one would usually find in cities, and especially the larger cities. It is not unknown for several dozen or more households to use the same pipe or well, or to wash dishes or clean food in drainage ditches. Also not unknown are waterborne diseases spread by those using wells, standpipes and drainage ditches.

As noted above, most governments place a high priority on providing quality drinking water for their citizens. These programs are also among the highest on the lists for international aid. Governments recognize that quality water is a basic human need that will not only improve the overall health and longevity of residents, but lead to a healthier economy and raise the overall living standards for rural and urban residents.

Environmental issues

Central Eurasia faces a number of environmental issues, of which the major ones are depicted on Map 29. Some of these are related to population pressures in areas of fragile environments, such as the steppes and deserts and alpine areas. In these areas the problem is one of expanding croplands into areas of low rainfall, the result of developing plow agriculture in places which are better suited for extensive pastoral economies. Desertification is the term used to describe the expanding desert lands. This problem is especially acute in the arid and semiarid regions of Mongolia, Xinjiang, Kazakhstan and also southern Central Asian states. Agricultural economies are not the only ones affected by plowing up areas with thin soils; expanding city populations are affected as well. Water, even for those

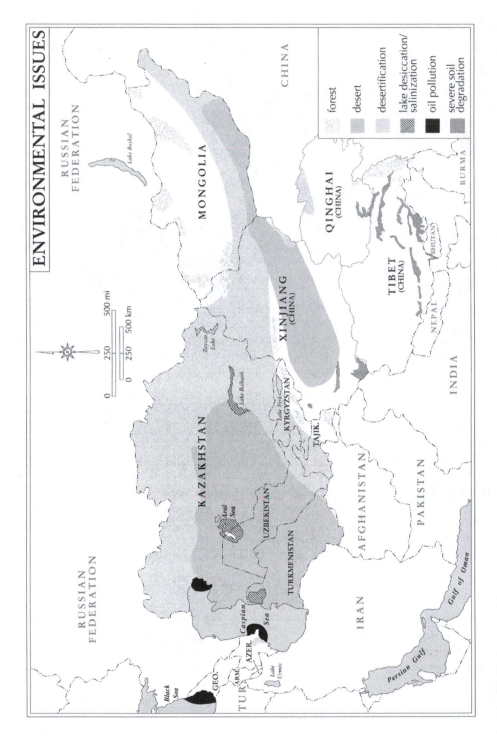

ENVIRONMENTAL ISSUES

Legend

- forest
- desert
- desertification
- lake desiccation/ salinization
- oil pollution
- severe soil degradation

RUSSIAN FEDERATION

RUSSIAN FEDERATION

CHINA

MONGOLIA

Lake Baikal

QINGHAI (CHINA)

XINJIANG (CHINA)

TIBET (CHINA)

BURMA

NEPAL

BHUTAN

INDIA

Zaysan Lake

KAZAKHSTAN

Lake Balkash

KYRGYZSTAN

Lake Yssk

TAJIK.

Aral Sea

UZBEKISTAN

TURKMENISTAN

AFGHANISTAN

PAKISTAN

Caspian Sea

IRAN

Gulf of Oman

Persian Gulf

Black Sea

GEO.

TUR

ARM.

AZER.

Lake Urmia

0   250   500 mi

0   250   500 km

Map 29 Environmental issues

near a major river or a major mountain source, is still a precious commodity for cities where there are growing demands for residential and industrial use. Prime agricultural lands, because they are level and well drained, are also strong candidates for expanding urban residential, industrial and transportation land uses.

A second major issue is soil degradation, which is directly related to expanding plow agriculture into areas where it is an unwise and unsustainable practice. The already thin soil layer is also destroyed or removed by wind erosion, which is often a severe problem in much of rural Central Eurasia. The immediate results are lower crop productivity levels and, for areas with pastoral economies, acute land erosion due to overgrazing. Acute soil degradation is a major environmental issue not only in areas of extensive grain cultivation and livestock herding, but also in mountainous areas. Note especially on Map 29, the severe levels that exist in central and eastern Tibet and parts of Xinjiang.

A third problem is lake desiccation and salinization. The Aral Sea, which has been shrinking for the past fifty years, is one of the areas affected by these processes, but so are areas in the eastern Caspian Sea and Lake Balkash in eastern Kazakhstan. The Aral Sea shrinking is attributed to less water entering this inland lake, water which has its origins in the highlands of western China. The two major rivers entering the Aral Sea, the Amu Darya and Syr Darya, are major regions of irrigated crop agriculture for Uzbekistan in particular. When less water from these rivers flows into the Aral Sea, the result is a shrinking shoreline. Less water is then available for agriculture and for the many high density farming communities nearby. Many environmental groups in the past several decades have used the Aral Sea shrinking to call attention to the region's severe ecological problems. Stranded boats on former shorelines, huge salt flats and abandoned river courses are images many have of this region. Related environmental problems not shown on the map are the short- and long-term impacts of heavy applications of fertilizers and pesticides which are all designed to increase cotton production especially. A variety of health problems affect those along these rivers, not only from the groundwater they use, but from the occasional strong winds which also carry pollutants.

A fourth set of problems is associated with points, not areas; these are cities and industrial areas. Oil pollution of waters is associated with western Georgia and production areas around Baku and Atyrau. Oil and gas economies, while bringing income and growth to these areas, also befoul the air and water and can lead to unhealthy conditions for children and adults. Not shown on the map, again because of scale, are other urban areas in Central Eurasia from Mongolia to the Caucasus where there are heavy industrial complexes, often located in city centers, which pose environmental risk to populations near the plants or mining regions, but also to those downstream and downwind. Pollutants can be lead, zinc, titanium and also cement, steel, paper, and chemical plants.

The final set of environmental problems is associated with diminished forest cover. Deforestation is especially a severe problem in mountainous areas where the population densities are high. Examples of these are in rural Tibet, northern Mongolia, eastern Kyrgyzstan and southeast Tajikistan. Wood here is used both as a fuel for cooking and as a source of heat in the winter seasons. The results of cutting firewood are the same in these locations as in other parts of the world where deforestation is a serious environmental problem: avalanches, serious erosion of croplands and forestlands, and downriver flooding. It is not unknown for communities and agricultural areas downstream from heavily deforested areas to be destroyed or severely damaged by unwise forest cutting in highland areas upstream.

Earthquakes

Earthquakes are almost a daily occurrence in the Pamirs, Caucasus and Himalayan region. These can be light or mild tremors that are considered commonplace by many locals, who continue going about their business whether farming, working in factories or office buildings, or going to and from work. They are so commonplace that for many they are not even mentioned in casual conversations. Many that occur in sparsely populated rural areas are not even recorded or considered important news items.

There are, however, occasions when the earthquakes are severe and cause extensive damage, especially in large cities. They cause damage not only to residential, industrial and commercial areas, but to transportation, power generating and municipal water systems. Among the most devastating earthquakes last century were the quakes in Ashgabat in 1948 and Tashkent in 1966. Within the past decade there have been major earthquakes in Kyrgyzstan, Tajikistan and also Xinjiang, China, all measuring about 5.5 in magnitude. Specific areas that are prone to serious earthquakes are all three states in the Caucasus, but especially Armenia and Azerbaijan, eastern Uzbekistan and adjacent parts of southern Kyrgyzstan and the Pamir region of Tajikistan, and also China's three western provinces.

Devastation in large cities receive the most national, regional and international attention. When earthquakes of a magnitude of 6.0 or higher occur in rural and isolated areas, they seldom receive the same coverage. International relief efforts (food, medicine and housing) are more likely to come to urban areas that are devastated than to the countryside or sparsely populated areas. The 2010 Yushu earthquake in Qinghai registered 6.9 and killed more than 2,500. Note should also be made that there are vast areas of Kazakhstan, especially in the north, where earthquakes are a rarity. Here there are other natural disasters, such as prolonged summer drought, very high summer temperatures or extended periods of bitter cold weather in the winter.

The shrinking Aral Sea

One of the planet's major ecocatastrophes is the shrinking Aral Sea, not just because it is shrinking, but because of what that means to the populations living in and around it. A map of the sea in 1957 showed a body of water (actually more a lake than a sea) with just a few small islands. Twenty years later the shrinking became more apparent, especially with coastlines changing in the eastern and northern portions. Images of derelict towns and graveyards of fishing vessels were shown worldwide. It must be remembered that the sea has always been shallow (in the early twentieth century the depth was 70 m or 230 ft). The shrinking has not been because of climate change in this Central Asian region, but because more water was diverted for productive cotton economies and because the Chinese release less water into the rivers, the Syr Darya from the north and the Amu Darya from the south.

The shrinking has continued during the past couple of decades. Note both the changes in the shoreline and also the appearance of more land that was once below the surface of the water. Islands that were once small and few have now been connected as part of a land surface. A further note on the islands is another important part of the Aral Sea story. The sea and the islands are on a major fly-way of birds migrating into Russia from southern and southwestern Asia. In short, the island was a major area of biodiversity. The shrinking of the sea means that many are probably flying over the sea now and going to major nesting places farther north. Also the islands in the Aral were used as a toxic dump site during Soviet years. Many residents in areas near the Aral Sea did not know this, nor did most

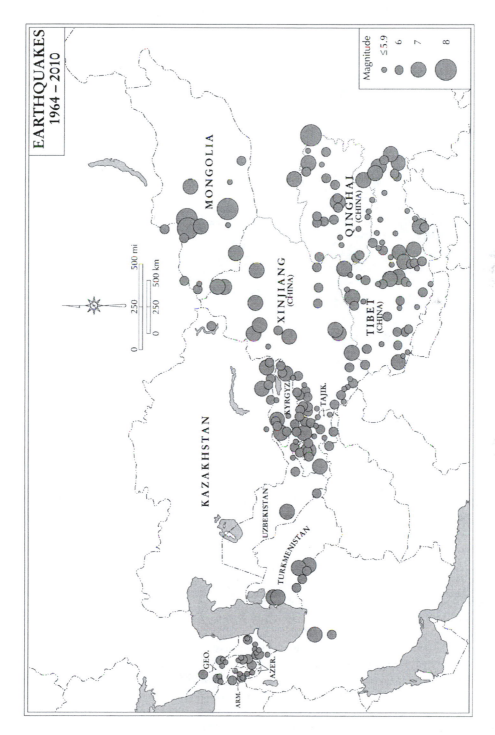

Map 30 Earthquakes 1964–2010

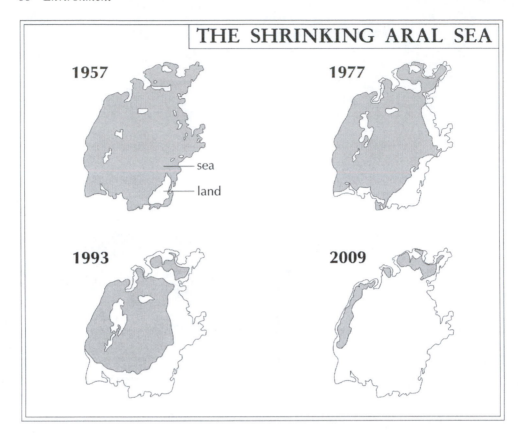

Figure 7 The shrinking Aral Sea

Central Asians. The fact was not publicized. It would not be surprising if many migratory birds consuming water or insects in and around the Aral Sea were contaminated and likely carried diseases with them to their new habitats and transferred them to their offspring.

The shrinking is likely to continue as there seems to be no compelling reason to believe it will expand again to its 1950s area. With the help of the Kazakh government and the World Bank the 13 km (8 mile) Kok-Aral dam was constructed in the northern part of the sea in 2005. It was designed to raise the level in this northern area; fish were also reintroduced into the sea in hopes of gradually increasing fish production. The North Aral Sea has recovered somewhat and is receiving water from the Syr Darya. The South Aral Sea, however, no longer receives water from the Amu Darya; thus the likelihood of the complete desiccation of the South Aral Sea is much greater. The long-term result of the desiccation will likely be the complete disappearance of the lake in the next three decades. If this occurs, the area will become, like that around it, a region of continued wind erosion, acute health problems for residents dependent on the two rivers for drinking water and irrigated agriculture, and likely farm abandonment (already occurring) and rural depopulation. In short, this is an ecocatastrophe in the region. Evidence of the shrinking of the Aral Sea, the emerging coastlines and the abandoned river channels is already visible from flying over the area or accessing maps from Google Earth.

6 Economic

Arable land

The single most important feature about arable land in Central Eurasia is that there is very little. Arable land is land that can be used for agriculture, that is, crop and/or livestock production. The paucity of such land in Central Eurasia is clearly emphasized in the three categories in Map 31. This figure is also deceptive when mapping the percentage of arable land, in our case by country. What the map does not illustrate is the very, very small patches of arable land in much of the region.

Kazakhstan is shown as having more than 15 percent of all land that is arable. That 15 percent is mostly concentrated in the Virgin Lands in the northern third of the country, an area adjacent to Russia. Even in this region which is important for grain production, high annual yields are far from common. More likely, as one would expect in any region

Map 31 Arable land, 2007

of semiarid and arid climates, there would be periods of ample rainfall interspersed with periods of less than sufficient amounts of moisture. Cool spring temperatures and early frosts also shorten the growing season.

The major subregion with a productive agricultural economy is the Caucasus, where one can find intensive crop (fruits) and vegetable production and also livestock economies providing food for the nearby local populations. A much smaller productive region is the Fergana Valley in southern Kyrgyzstan and adjacent Uzbekistan which is not only a major cotton-producing area, but also a major supplier of fruits and vegetables for much of urban and small city Uzbekistan, Kyrgyzstan and Kazakhstan. It is not unusual to find southern Central Asian produce in cities in northern Kazakhstan where it arrives in huge truck caravans for weekly bazaars.

The paucity of productive agricultural areas for crops is evidenced by the huge areas on the map where less than 5 percent of the land is under the plow. Most of Uzbekistan and Turkmenistan are arid and semiarid, while much of Kyrgyzstan and Tajikistan are mountainous. Irregular terrain, inhospitable climates, thin soils and absence of moisture are characteristic of much of Mongolia and the western Chinese provinces. Oasis agriculture is found around small cities and settlements where there is sufficient water for productive seasonal crops: grains, fruits and vegetables.

Cultivated land

This category includes land that can actually be used for cultivating crops, that is, land that is under the plow. As in the case of the previous map, when considering the region from Georgia to Mongolia and China's three western provinces, it is evident that only a

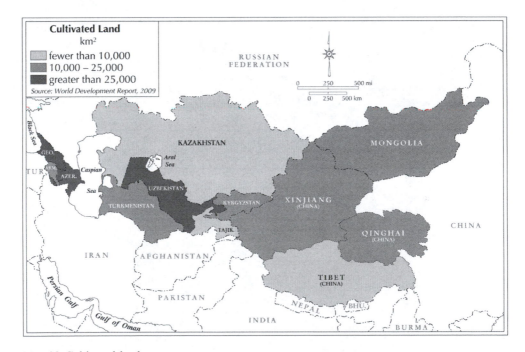

Map 32 Cultivated land

very small percentage is cultivated land (Map 32). In regards to individual countries, there is less than 6,037 square miles (10,000 km²) of cultivated land in Kazakhstan, Tibet and Tajikistan. Most of Kazakhstan, as previous maps show, faces extremely harsh environmental conditions for growing crops. The cropland regions are the steppe region in the country's north, which has a good *chernozem* soil base, and. in the south, the flat lands and well-watered valleys near the Kyrgyz border.

Map 32 must be read with some caution as it also shows the amount of agricultural land in each country and Chinese province; it does not show where that productive area actually is. This confusion is in evidence when we consider Uzbekistan, which along with Azerbaijan and Georgia, has the largest amount of cultivated land. Azerbaijan and Georgia have very intensive areas of productive cropland agriculture; in fact, these countries have a high population density and high percentage of land devoted to raising grains and subtropical crops. Uzbekistan, on the other hand, has vast areas of harsh environmental conditions, not only adjacent to the Aral Sea, but it also has a very high agricultural density in the Fergana Valley, which will place this country in the same category as the two Caucasus countries. Like subtropical Georgia and Azerbaijan, the subtropical Fergana Valley produces fresh fruits and vegetables for urban economies nearby and also distant from Samarkand, Tashkent and Osh.

The cultivated areas in much of Turkmenistan, Tajikistan, Mongolia, Xinjiang and Tibet are associated with areas where there are good soils and ample water supplies for intensive crop production. Many of these areas would appear as isolated urban and agricultural patches or islands, if we mapped places of high crop productivity.

Poverty rate

The proportion of a population that is poor is always a tricky index to calculate and also to map. Poverty defines those who are poor, but defining what makes a person poor will vary with the country gathering and tabulating such data or international organizations seeking ways to provide some degree of comparability. The World Development Index, developed by the United Nations, provides an aggregate figure for countries in Central Eurasia; it identifies the proportion of those in the population who are considered poor. That value varies considerably, as one might expect, from less than 20 percent in two of the Caucasus states (Georgia and Azerbaijan) to more than 70 percent in Uzbekistan, Mongolia and the Tibetan Autonomous Region in China. In between these two extremes are the other countries and Chinese provinces.

What is most unfortunate when looking at the poverty variable for Central Eurasia is that there are no finer data available for geographical units below the states themselves. That is, there are no smaller census or administrative unit areas in Turkmenistan or Azerbaijan or Kazakhstan that provide data on those who are poor; such finer scales of data collecting and analysis exist in many other countries where there are more data on population numbers, employment and quality of life of those who are considered poor.

What can be stated with some degree of certainty by those who have first-hand familiarity with the region is that there are some significant differences between the urban and rural poor. Per capita incomes are usually lower in rural areas, especially where agriculture is a mainstay of the economy. High incomes may exist in regions where there is some valuable mineral extracted or a major industrial site produces some high-value finished product. Incomes are generally higher in urban areas, not only because the skill and education levels are higher than in rural areas, but because living costs are also higher. Throughout

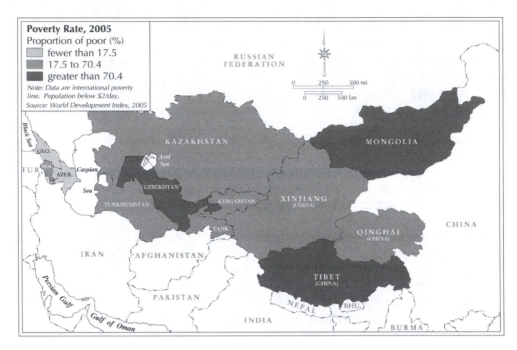

Map 33 Poverty rate, 2005

rural Central Eurasia one could find some agricultural areas where the standard of living and quality of life is very low and where the level may even approach a subsistence (living off the land) level. In urban areas, and especially in the large capital cities and major industrial centers, the incomes will be higher for professionals, semiprofessionals, and even day laborers. In many cities, especially capital cities in the region that have boomed with recent economic or good investments, one can find expensive car dealers, new single-dwellings and gated communities, and also stores selling costly consumer items and products for an elite and potentially growing middle class. However, these same cities may also be the destinations of rural inhabitants and the poor who consider an urban move as an opportunity to get out of a perpetual cycle of poverty for their families and friends.

Mineral deposits

Industrial and energy minerals, by their very existence, have an uneven distribution. That is, the concentrations are associated with where they have been discovered and can be mined extensively. This statement applies just as much to the locations of oil and gas discussed below as to coal, iron, lead, zinc, gold, silver and other valuable industrial commodities. Not infrequently large deposits of ores are the sites of major industrial centers, which may also be major political, administrative and transportation centers, or there may be industrial centers nearby.

Two distinguishing features appear on Map 34. First, is the large number of valuable minerals found in Kazakhstan, which makes it, not surprisingly, the major center for a variety of major mineral economies in Central Eurasia. Copper, lead and zinc are mined in northeast Kazakhstan, copper, iron and manganese in the center, and gold, iron and

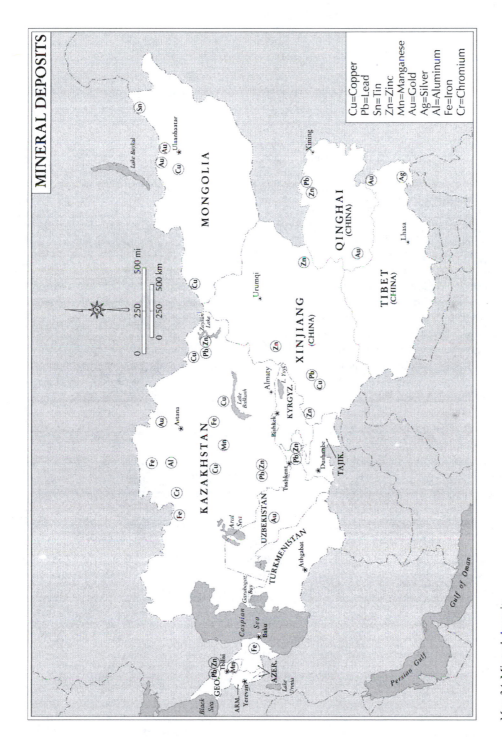

MINERAL DEPOSITS

Cu=Copper
Pb=Lead
Sn=Tin
Zn=Zinc
Mn=Manganese
Au=Gold
Ag=Silver
Al=Aluminum
Fe=Iron
Cr=Chromium

MONGOLIA

QINGHAI
(CHINA)

TIBET
(CHINA)

XINJIANG
(CHINA)

KAZAKHSTAN

UZBEKISTAN

TURKMENISTAN

KYRGYZ.

TAJIK.

AZER.

ARM.

GEO.

Ulaanbaatar

Xining

Lhasa

Urumqi

Astana

Almaty

Bishkek

Tashkent

Dushanbe

Ashgabat

Baku

Tbilisi

Yerevan

Lake Baikal

Zaysan Lake

Lake Balkash

L. Yssyk

Aral Sea

Caspian Sea

Garabogaz Buy

Lake Urmia

Black Sea

Persian Gulf

Gulf of Oman

500 mi
500 km
0   250   500
0   250   500

Map 34 Mineral deposits

chromium in the north near the Russian border. Scattered deposits of several minerals are associated with small towns and cities in Georgia, northeast Mongolia and eastern Uzbekistan. While there are not many minerals located on the map in Tibet and Qinghai, there are reports of reserves of gold, chromite, uranium and copper. Xinjiang has coal, iron ore, copper and nickel as well as oil and natural gas.

Noteworthy on Map 34 are "mineral voids," that is, places where there are few if any major industrial minerals. These include Turkmenistan, Tajikistan, Kyrgyzstan and Armenia. If one prepared a map that combined the locations of major industrial mineral deposits and major oil and gas fields, the concentrations in Kazakhstan would be the most striking and clearly would illustrate that this country has the greatest variety of mineral economies within its borders and also the greatest reserves.

Oil fields and pipelines

A major source of income for several states in the region, specifically Kazakhstan, Uzbekistan, Turkmenistan and Azerbaijan, comes from the production of oil and gas.

These countries in fact have some of the richest deposits of these minerals of any in Asia. They are concentrated in several major locations: the Caspian Sea areas around Baku, Azerbaijan and around Aktau and Atyrau in western Kazakhstan. Both countries have deep deposits of oil, which are not only mined on land, but extend into the Caspian Sea itself. This observation is apparent on the map. The Caspian is not a deep water body where mining occurs. The decades-old fields, especially in and around Baku, have been around for nearly a century and are major driving forces for both regional and national economies. More recently rich oil and gas fields were discovered in eastern and central Turkmenistan which are major revenue sources for the government in this basically desert country. China has oil fields in Xinjiang and Qinghai. Xinjiang has become the new oil center for China. The Karamay fields in northern Xinjiang have been pumping since 1958. Karamay means black oil in Uyghur. The Tarim Basin oil fields which also include natural gas have been developed since the 1990s.

The demand for Central Eurasian oil and gas is greatest, as we would expect, in regions where fossil fuel deposits are meager or absent. Most of the oil and gas from this region is sent through an intricate set of pipelines under the Caspian Sea through the Caucasus states to Central European countries or through pipeline systems into, through and across Russia. Many of these pipelines, especially in Kazakhstan and Turkmenistan, are constructed over long distances from production fields to industrial and commercial centers inside and outside the region. China and Kazakhstan jointly constructed a pipeline which brings Kazakhstani oil to Xinjiang and on to the rest of China. China also has a natural gas pipeline out to Xinjiang and another natural gas pipeline links Turkmenistan to China via Uzbekistan and Kazakhstan.

One further striking feature of the oil and gas fields is the absence of these deposits in much of Central Eurasia. Large populated areas in western China, northern Kazakhstan and the Caucasus region are not associated with these hydrocarbons.

Caspian oil fields

As one would expect, there are competing claims to deposits in the Caspian Sea itself. Russia and Kazakhstan are the states with the longest coastlines and access to rich oil fields. Maps have been drawn that show claims of states bordering the Caspian Sea to the deposits

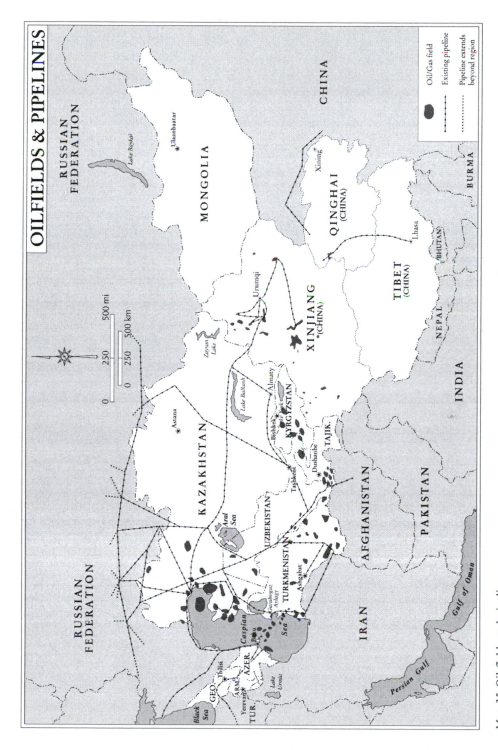

Map 35 Oil fields and pipelines

Map 36 Caspian Sea oil and gas

beneath the waters. One of the underlying legal issues here is whether the Caspian is a sea or a lake. It is commonly referred to as a sea, but actually it is a lake, that is, an inland water body with no access to a larger body of water that it drains into.

Oil in the Caspian Sea Region accounts for a significant amount of global reserves after the Persian Gulf region and Russia. The main centers of production in the Caspian are in Kazakhstan (Tengiz and Karachagnak fields) and Azerbaijan (Azeri, Chirag and Gunashi fields). Offshore oil production in Azerbaijan began in the 1870s. Russia and Turkmenistan have some oil production from the Caspian. Production is developing in the Caspian area and is currently at the level of Venezuela. Pipelines from Baku go toward Turkey (via Georgia) and Russia. From Kazakhstan's Caspian fields, pipelines go to Russia and China.

Manufacturing/industrial sites

Three significant patterns emerge when looking at the distribution of manufacturing or industrial sites in Central Eurasia. First are the concentrations in the largest cities, which in most cases are also the capital cities. Examples include Tashkent, Baku, Bishkek, Dushanbe, Yerevan and Tbilisi. The development of heavy and light industrial economies is not unexpected in these cities, since they are also major centers for highways and rail lines and now air links. The history of these industrial economies, whether oil and gas refining, steel, chemicals, motor vehicles, agricultural and mining equipment, food processing or textiles, goes back to Soviet days, in the case of former republics of the USSR. In the case of China, the industrial centers in the three provinces in western China, Urumqi, Lhasa and Xining, trace their industrial economies to government programs in frontier areas. For example, Urumqi has a petrochemical industry based on Xinjiang's oil deposits and a cotton processing industry. Indeed Xinjiang's development strategy was referred to as black and white, that is, oil and cotton.

Second are those centers which are strongly associated with a single industry. Examples include the oil and gas economies associated with Baku, Azerbaijan and also Aktau and Atyrau on the Caspian Sea, iron and steel with Karaganda, Kazakhstan, and chemical plants in Ust-Kamenogorsk (or Oskemen) in northeast Kazakhstan.

Third are many of the smaller industrial centers associated with specific industries. Overall, the distribution of manufacturing and industrial sites is, not surprisingly, similar to that of population density, that is, the areas with the densest highway, rail and air traffic.

Transportation

The major historical route across this region, as noted above, was the Silk Road, which was not a single road, but rather a combination of routes that crisscrossed the steppes and deserts linking some of the earliest villages and cities and those near major sources of water.

There are five outstanding features about the surface transportation networks in greater Central Eurasia. First, there is no major intricate or extensive system of highways that covers the region. Rather there is often one major highway that links major cities, usually the capitals, and important secondary regional centers. This feature is easily discerned from the major highway map (Map 38). Second, the highway pattern basically is one associated with population density, which is not surprising. Thus, the pattern is one with denser patterns on the periphery than in the center. Note the dense networks in southeastern Kazakhstan and northern Kyrgyzstan and, of course, the Caucasus states. Third, there are vast areas of this region which are not covered by good surfaced highways; these are mostly inhospitable

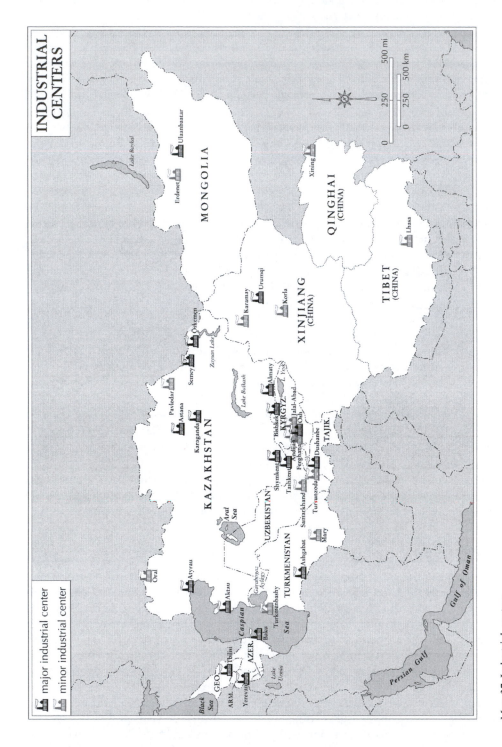

Map 37 Industrial centers

TRANSPORTATION

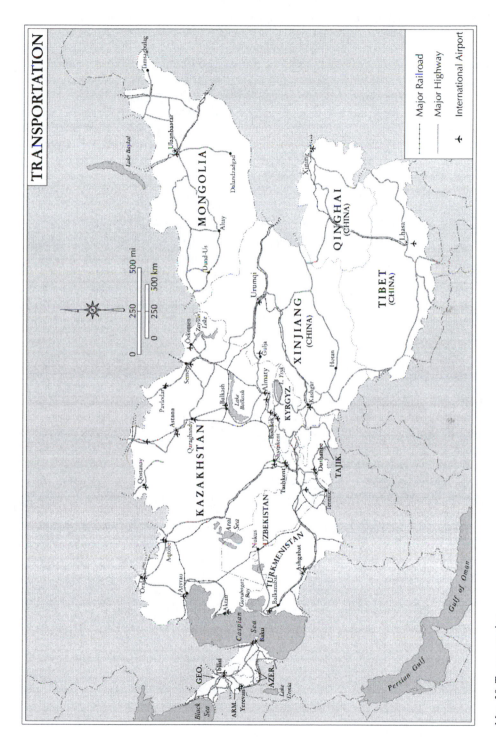

Major Railroad
Major Highway
✈ International Airport

Map 38 Transportation

areas and harshlands, for example, the Tibetan Plateau, mountainous western China, most of Mongolia and the huge desert area that includes Kazakhstan and adjacent Uzbekistan and Turkmenistan. Fourth, most of the region is poorly served by railroads. In fact, there are many cities not served extensively by major railroads. Most travelers will use buses to travel short and long distances. Fifth, there are huge distances between some of the major and minor cities linked in the region. The settlement patterns and road densities are, not surprisingly, higher in the Caucasus, in the Fergana Valley, and in the Bishkek–Almaty corridor. Elsewhere there are few if any linking roads in much of western China, central and northern Kazakhstan and western Uzbekistan, Turkmenistan and Kazakhstan. The places that are linked are capitals and major industrial centers. Distances are long between even many places that are on the major highways. Smaller places, especially off major roads and not shown on the maps, would be much more inaccessible.

Another illustration of the region's peripheral population patterns is provided by the international airports. These are mostly in major industrial and/or capital cities. All the Central Eurasian cities are served by international airports, some served by flights originating in Istanbul, Amsterdam and Moscow and others from Beijing and Shanghai. The international airlines serving these capital cities bring in local business and government leaders, tourists and some students; these are some of the same groups that travel to nearby or distant Russian, Chinese, South Asian or European cities. Residents in capital cities clearly have a greater variety of ways to travel than those in large and small regional centers. Buses are extensively used for internal travel and many regularly serve medium-sized and even smaller urban locations.

Imports/exports

The nine states in Central Eurasia exported more than US $134 billion worth of products in 2008 and imported $79 billion. (This figure does not include the three Chinese provinces.) The leading exporter, by value, was Kazakhstan which exported nearly $72 billion, or 53 percent of the total exports of these nine states. Azerbaijan was a distant second with $31 billion. The next leading exporting countries were Turkmenistan and Uzbekistan with $12 billion and $10 billion respectively. At the other end of the spectrum were Kyrgyzstan, Tajikistan and Armenia with $1.8 billion, $1.5 billion and $1.1 billion in exports respectively.

The major importing countries are, not surprisingly, the leading exporting countries. Kazakhstan accounts for nearly half of the imports of these nine countries; Uzbekistan is second with only 12 percent of the total and Azerbaijan third with only 10 percent. Armenia, Kyrgyzstan, Tajikistan and Mongolia together account for 18 percent of all imports. Many of the same products exported are also those imported. Machinery and equipment are the leading imports for Kazakhstan, Azerbaijan, Turkmenistan and Uzbekistan. For Kyrgyzstan, Georgia and Armenia fuels are high on the list. Various food products are imported by all countries.

The major exports in dollar value from the region were, not surprisingly from what we have observed above, minerals and manufactured goods as well as oil and gas products. Ninety percent of Azerbaijan's exports are oil and gas and for Kazakhstan the proportion is 59 percent. For Turkmenistan and Uzbekistan the percentages are much lower. Ferrous metals (iron ore, gold, copper, etc.), machinery, chemicals and motor vehicles are also major exports from the more industrial countries. Agricultural products (cotton, wool, tobacco and foodstuffs) are leading exports for Armenia, Tajikistan, Mongolia and Georgia.

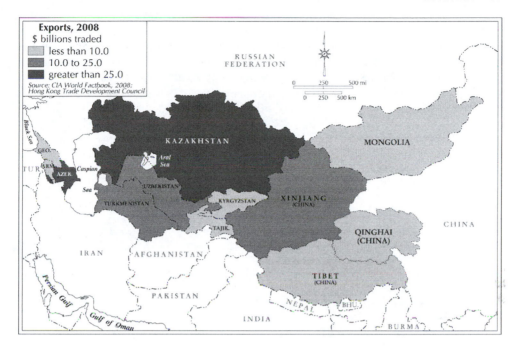

Map 39 Exports, 2008

Map 40 Imports, 2008

In regards to major trading partners, the most distinguishing feature of the region is the continued influence, even dominance of Russia. Many of the trading agreements that existed during the Soviet Union remain intact. Russia was the leading importing country for all nine Central Eurasian countries except Georgia, which is understandable considering their recent border conflict. Georgia's leading importing country was Turkey. One-third of Kazakhstan's imports came from Russia, for Mongolia it was 38 percent and for Kyrgyzstan

MONGOLIA
2008 exports
($2.54 billion)

copper, apparel, livestock, animal products,
cashmere, wool, hides, fluorospar, other
nonferrous metals, coal

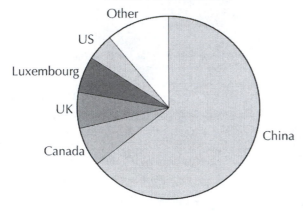

MONGOLIA
2008 imports
($3.22 billion)

machinery and equipment, fuel, automobiles,
food products, industrial consumer goods,
chemicals, building materials, sugar, tea

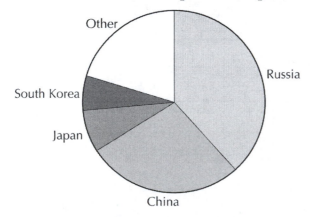

Figure 8 Trade: Mongolia

37 percent. China, which is the emerging economic power in Central Eurasia – an observation that is clearly discernible whether walking through bazaars or visiting many retail outlets – was the second leading importing nation. Various European countries were also among the top five sources of imports. For example, for Armenia, the second, third and fourth leading importing countries were Germany, Netherlands and Belgium; for Kazakhstan, they

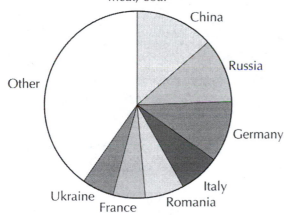

KAZAKHSTAN
2008 exports
($71.97 billion)

oil and oil products, ferrous metals,
chemicals, machinery, grain, wool,
meat, coal

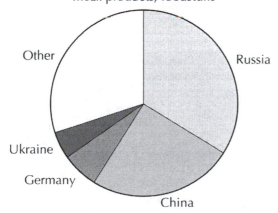

KAZAKHSTAN
2008 imports
($38.45 billion)

machinery and equipment,
metal products, foodstuffs

Figure 9 Trade: Kazakhstan

were China, Germany and Ukraine; and for Turkmenistan, they were China, Turkey and the UAE.

The leading exporting countries also varied as many of the leaders were dissimilar from the leading importing countries. Azerbaijan's second through fourth leading countries were Italy, the USA and Israel; for Kyrgyzstan they were Switzerland, Russia and Uzbekistan; for Kazakhstan they were Russia, Germany and Italy; and for Turkmenistan, the second and

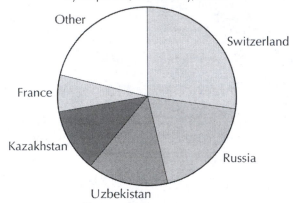

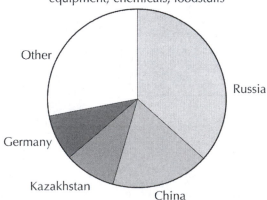

Figure 10 Trade: Kyrgyzstan

third were Poland and Hungary. One can observe from these rankings how dependent Central and Western Europe were on obtaining oil and gas from these leading Central Eurasian states.

Of the three Chinese provinces the leader by far was Xinjiang with US $19 billion in exports, most of which are in shoes, yarn and casings. Xinjiang's major trading partners are nearby Kazakhstan and Kyrgyzstan and Pakistan; Tibet's are Nepal, Japan and Hong Kong; and Qinghai's are Japan, the USA and South Korea.

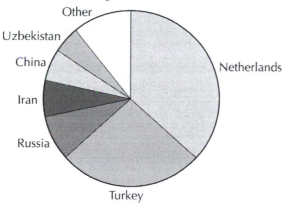

TAJIKISTAN
2008 exports
($1.58 billion)
aluminum, electricity, cotton, fruits, vegetable oil, textiles

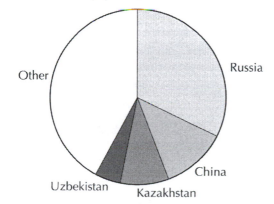

TAJIKISTAN
2008 imports
($3.7 billion)
electricity, petroleum products, aluminum oxide, machinery and equipment, foodstuffs

Figure 11 Trade: Tajikistan

UZBEKISTAN
2008 exports
($10.3 billion)

natural gas, oil, cotton, gold, mineral fertilizers,
ferrous and nonferrous metals, textiles, food
products, machinery, automobiles

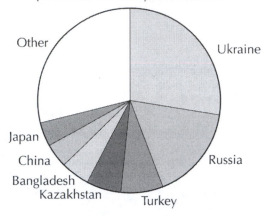

UZBEKISTAN
2008 imports
($9.28 billion)

machinery and equipment, foodstuffs,
chemicals, ferrous and nonferrous metals

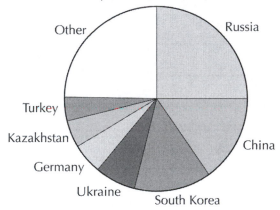

Figure 12 Trade: Uzbekistan

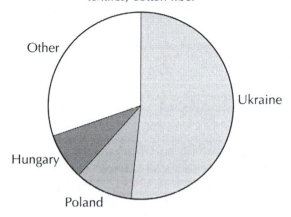

TURKMENISTAN
2008 exports
($12.34 billion)
gas, crude oil, petrochemicals,
textiles, cotton fiber

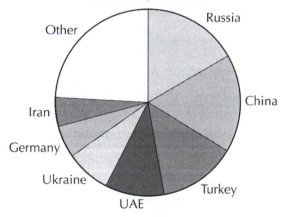

TURKMENISTAN
2008 imports
($5.6 billion)
machinery and equipment,
chemicals, foodstuffs

Figure 13 Trade: Turkmenistan

AZERBAIJAN
2008 exports
($30.59 billion)
oil and gas (90%), machinery,
cotton, foodstuffs

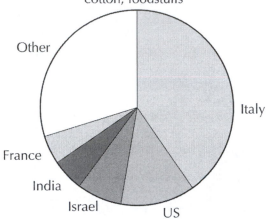

AZERBAIJAN
2008 imports
($7.58 billion)
machinery and equipment, oil products,
foodstuffs, metals, chemicals

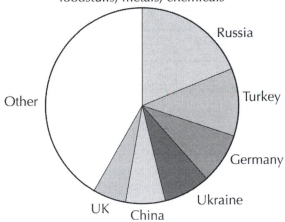

Figure 14 Trade: Azerbaijan

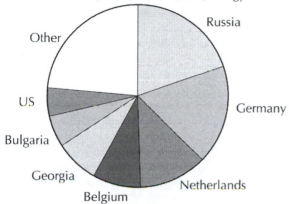

ARMENIA
2008 exports
($1.124 billion)

pig iron, copper, nonferrous metals,
diamonds, minerals, foodstuffs, energy

Russia

Other

US

Germany

Bulgaria

Georgia

Belgium

Netherlands

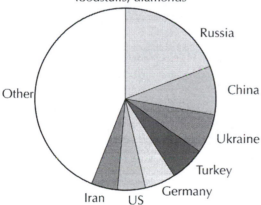

ARMENIA
2008 imports
($3.73 billion)

natural gas, petroleum, tobacco,
foodstuffs, diamonds

Russia

Other

China

Ukraine

Turkey

Iran   US   Germany

Figure 15 Trade: Armenia

GEORGIA
2008 exports
($2.43 billion)

scrap metal, wine, mineral water,
ores, vehicles, fruits, nuts

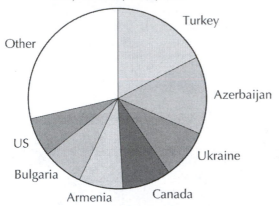

GEORGIA
2008 imports
($6.26 billion)

fuels, vehicles, machinery, grain,
other foods, pharmaceuticals

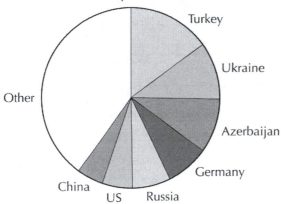

Figure 16 Trade: Georgia

Foreign direct investment

Foreign direct investment (FDI) is investment in the domestic economy coming from abroad. Much of the global foreign direct investment in Central Eurasia is from the USA, Europe and Japan. When comparing FDI as a percentage of GDP, Mongolia, Tajikistan and Georgia had higher ratios over 10 percent, while Kazakhstan, Kyrgyzstan, Turkmenistan and Armenia are at the 5–10 percent level. China has a high ratio in general, but of the western provinces in Central Eurasia only Xinjiang registers much foreign direct investment.

If we measure foreign direct investment in terms of net inflows in 2006, Kazakhstan was a clear leader with US $6 billion in investment. Georgia had $1 billion and Turkmenistan $730 million, while all other countries had FDI of less than $350 million. In 2009, after the global recession and the Georgia–Russia conflict, Kazakhstan attracted $16 billion in FDI, Turkmenistan generated over $1 billion in FDI, and all other countries generated less than $750 million in FDI. The biggest generator of FDI then seems to be the oil sectors of the economy in Kazakhstan and Turkmenistan.

The currencies of the states include the Chinese *yuan* and the Mongolian *tugrik*. In Central Asia the currencies are as follows: Kazakhstan *tenge,* Kyrgyzstan *som*, Tajikistan *somoni*, Turkmenistan *manta* and Uzbekistan *soum*. In the Caucasus, the currencies are the Armenian *dram*, Azerbaijan *manta* and Georgian *lari*.

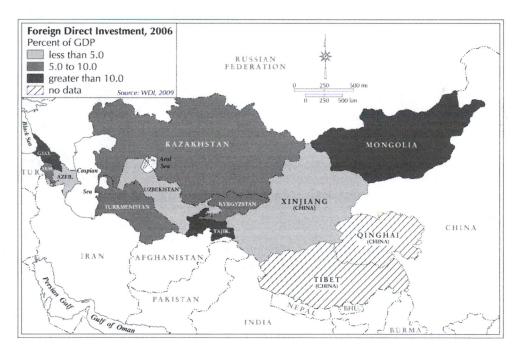

Map 41 Foreign direct investment, 2006

International tourism

The most recent international data on tourists arriving in Central Eurasia are from 2005. The accompanying figure compares the total incoming arrivals for 2000 and 2005. The clear leader is Kazakhstan, which attracted nearly 3 million visitors in 2005; Azerbaijan was a distant second with only one-third that amount. All other countries attracted fewer than 550,000 with the fewest visiting Qinghai and Tajikistan. Mongolia, Kyrgyzstan and Armenia attracted about 300,000 and Tibet a little over 100,000 in 2005.

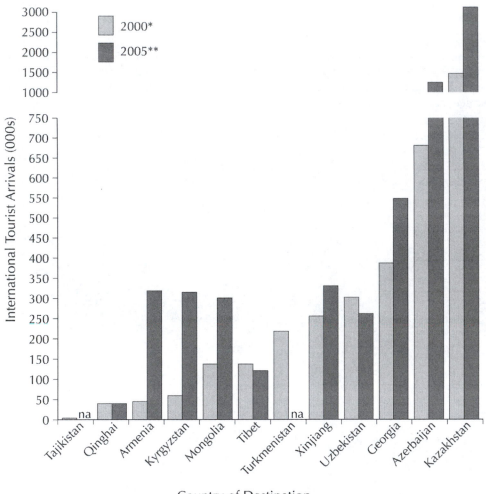

*1995 data for Turkmenistan, 2001 data for Tibet and Qinghai
**2004 data for Kazakhstan and Uzbekistan

Figure 17 International tourism

If we were provided specific details on the kinds of tourists who visited the region, they would be divided into at least two broad categories. First would be those who are tourists who visit places that only in the past decade have been popular for the global tourist population. These would mostly visit the largest cities, attend plays and national and regional sporting events as well as visit museums. Probably some of these visitors would attend tourist events alongside their diplomatic, educational or commercial visits. A second group would be the adventure tourists (some might consider all tourism venues in this region as adventures); they would be less likely to visit the major cultural centers, and more likely to hike, backpack and use buses and railroads to travel to little known destinations. For those inclined to this category of tourism, there is no shortage of possible places to visit from Mongolia to Georgia. Tourists would have to obtain visas to enter a country, and for those wishing to trek or climb in some parks or protected areas, additional permits would be required for individual or group excursions.

What is certain about tourism in this region is that many states and cities are investing resources to try and lure tourists from Japan, Europe, Australia and North America and also from among the growing middle classes in China itself. Evidence of this promotion is apparent on the official and unofficial websites of these Central Eurasian states, the promotion of unique physical landscapes and cultural events in travel offices in cities, and the translation of travel information into multiple languages.

It is very likely that tourism will continue to be a growing source of foreign revenue for this region. The construction of new hotels to meet western standards and the various packages promoted by travel agents inside and outside the region attest to the growing popularity of a region long excluded from the world tourism map. With new archaeological finds attracting the historical-minded tourist, the promotion of the Silk Road as a transnational experience and multiple adventure possibilities, the greater likelihood of major regional sporting events being held in major cities, and the opening of unique landscapes for the adventurous tourist, the future is indeed promising.

7 Cultural

Internet cafés

One criterion that can be used to discuss the degree of westernization or modernization in a city or country is the number of references to cybercafés or Internet cafés in major cities. This is not a perfect way to measure the impact of ICTs (information and communication technologies), but is a useful surrogate when more detailed and specific governmental and intergovernmental data are lacking.

Cybercafés or Internet cafés are places where computers are available for a wide range of uses and users. These include email, computer games and websites for personal or public use, and hobby and class uses. Internet cafés and Internet facilities are located in a wide variety of public places, including specific shops with only a few computers or banks of computers for personal use. They also include computers in corners of small shops, in bookstores, in hotel lobbies, in public libraries, airports, bus stations and other public places. Internet cafés dot the commercial landscapes of many central cities and major commercial streets and suburban shopping centers. In some cities one can find Internet clubs where most of the users are students working on class projects or children playing games. The popularity of Internet cafés is due to the fact that there are many youth and others who do not have personal computers or the ability to access the Internet from their homes. Hence, they will use cybercafés for one or more of the reasons given above.

The patterns shown on the map are almost certainly an incomplete picture of the actual number of Internet cafés in cities as it represents the number of references to such cafés. A detailed examination of the references would probably reveal Internet connections in libraries, hotels, travel agencies, universities, specific shops and also mentions in guidebooks for tourists and those in business. If we set any reservations aside, we discover, not surprisingly, that most references are to Internet cafés in the capital cities and the largest cities. In mid-2010 there were more than 50,000 references to Baku and Tashkent and from 30,000 to 50,000 in Lhasa (not surprising considering it is a major destination for various types of tourists) and Almaty (former capital of Kazakhstan, but still the major commercial center of the country for many international companies and organizations). Astana, Batumi (Georgia), Yerevan and Urumqui had around 10,000 references. Some capital cities had very few, for example, Bishkek, Dushanbe and Ashgabat. Uzbekistan and Kazakhstan are two countries where there was a good mix of these cafés in the larger, medium and smaller cities. Cities in Kazakhstan along the Caspian Sea, in the south bordering Uzbekistan and Kyrgyzstan, and in the north near the Russian border all had a good number of references to these Internet cafés. By contrast, the data source provided no references to small or medium-sized cities in Xinjiang, Qinghai, Tibet and Mongolia.

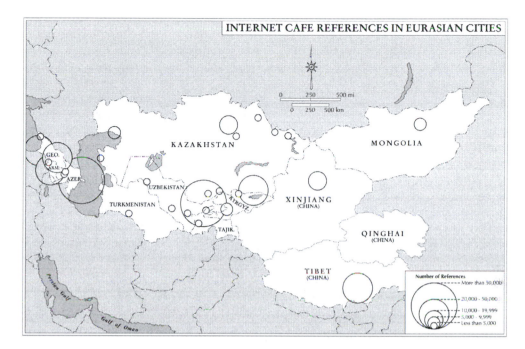

Map 42a Internet café references in Eurasian cities

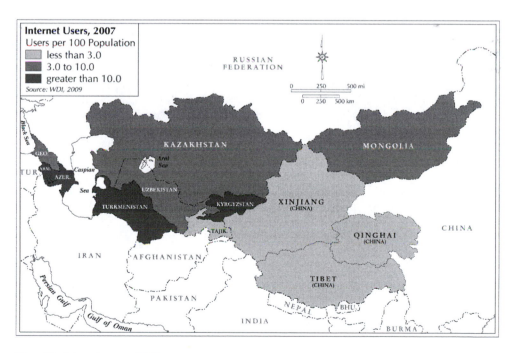

Map 42b Internet users, 2007

Universities

There are more than 275 colleges and universities in this region. These include long-established universities that can trace their roots back more than fifty years and new private universities, which are located primarily in the largest cities and capital cities. In addition to this number there are also many technical schools, military schools, business schools and presidential universities for those pursuing programs in the arts, sciences, medicine and law. Some of these are two-year programs, others four years or more where one can earn advanced degrees. Some of the private universities are very expensive; their faculty may include professors with international teaching experience or previous residence in the country.

The largest number of colleges and universities are in Kazakhstan, which has more than seventy. There are half that number in Uzbekistan, Kyrgyzstan, Georgia, Azerbaijan and Armenia. The fewest were in Mongolia, Xinjiang and Tibet.

There are more than twenty universities in Baku, Yerevan, Tbilisi, Almaty and Bishkek, and more than ten in Tashkent and Dushanbe. As noted above, most of these colleges, universities and technical schools are in the capital cities, where they attract students from throughout the country. In all Central Eurasian states one can find colleges and technical schools in many large and small regional centers. For example, there are twenty cities in Kazakhstan that have one to four colleges and universities, ten such cities in Uzbekistan and six in Azerbaijan. There are few colleges and universities outside the capital cities in Mongolia, Xinjiang, Turkmenistan and Tibet.

The end of the Soviet Union brought about changes in the colleges and universities in the former Soviet republics. Three major changes were the emergence of private colleges

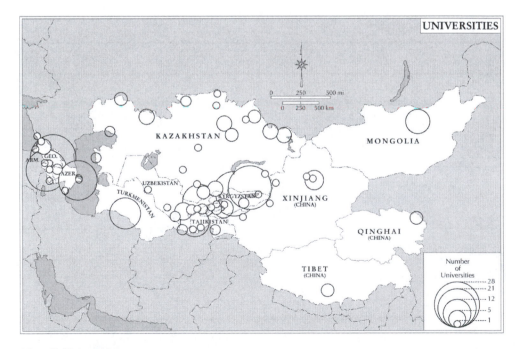

Map 43 Universities

and universities, some of which are very expensive for in-country students; the replacement of many Russian professors and administrators with majority titled ethnic populations; and the development of new curricula, separate from what existed during the Soviet period. Many universities developed curricula and degree programs based on western university models. There are numerous examples where large and small universities, and also private ones, have developed cooperative exchange programs with European and American universities. University partnerships with public and private colleges and universities have changed the higher education landscape of the arts and sciences. The current generation of students is trained in both subject matter and technical fields that are much different from those of their parents' generations. Scholarships are often available for the best qualified students, who, upon earning their international degrees in the West, are often required to return to their country of origin.

Museums

Eurasian states are proud of their heritage, as one can detect from a visit to any museums in the capital cities, which is where most museums are located. This city, in the case of the former Soviet Union, was the most important cultural center for each Soviet republic. All the republics had Lenin museums, often with a huge statue of Lenin in front of or at the side of the museum. Inside there would be many displays about Lenin and the Soviet period, sometimes covering two of the three or four floors. The demise of the Soviet Union changed many cultural features of these capital cities, including the names of the museums (now usually a name reflecting the nationality, not Soviet heritage). The museums now contain more materials about the new state's history and less about Lenin and the Soviet period, the spaces devoted to which will have been drastically reduced from two decades earlier. All national museums are state projects and reflect the image that the state chooses to project, whether including in its displays artifacts, archaeological treasures, maps, photos or other materials, both for its own residents and outsiders.

Many capital cities have a dozen or more museums; there are more than twenty each in Baku, Tbilisi and Yerevan. There are fewer than a dozen in major cities in southern Central Asia and western China. The museums are of many different types, including ethnographic museums, art galleries and natural science museums. and often there are special museums erected in honor of specific individuals or important military, religious (now, but not during Soviet days) and national events. Semey, Kazakhstan, where the Soviet Union detonated nuclear weapons for fifty years, has museums for Abai, a noted historical figure, and Dostoyevsky, an ethnographic museum and also a display in the medical college reflecting human abnormalities resulting from nuclear testing. The capital, Astana, has a President's Museum and also a Museum of Modern Art. Shymkent, a city in southern Kazakhstan, has a Museum of Repression. Museums are popular places for locals, including school children. They are also promoted by local, regional and national tourist boards. And they are places where one can often purchase local art and crafts, including paintings, jewelry, pottery, facsimiles of maps and books on post-Soviet history.

Not shown on Map 44 are the many oblast museums in smaller cities. These have important cultural and natural science exhibits, which are popular for school children of all ages and also for visits by parents on weekends. Their content, like those in the capital cities, has also changed since the end of the Soviet Union. It is not unknown for many statues of Lenin to be collected and placed in some public park near the museum or major gathering point. In some places, they have been removed and even destroyed.

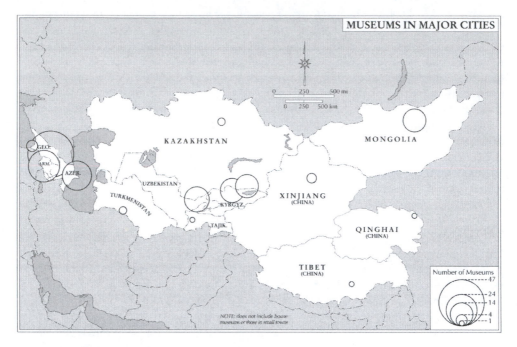

Map 44 Museums in major cities

Theaters

All capital cities have theaters and usually multiple theaters. The concentration of these cultural institutions is traced to Soviet days when these cities, especially, were the most important economic, educational, political and cultural centers of the republic. In some of the larger cities there are specific theaters for drama, ballet and even some for puppets and children. And there are multiple venues for music and concerts. For example, in Astana there is a Theater for Drama and Music, together with the State Theater of Russian Drama and the National Opera and Ballet Theater. Tashkent and Almaty, as two of the largest and most important cities in Central Eurasia, have eight and nine theaters respectively. According to the data source used to construct the map, which in all likelihood is incomplete, Urumqui, Baku and Ashgabat have two theaters, while there are one each in Lhasa, Ulaanbaatar, Yerevan and Dushanbe. Theaters and concert halls, like cinemas, are popular places for children, youth and adults on evenings and on weekends. Not shown on Map 45 are the many theaters in regional centers, which also are popular places for concerts, drama and other cultural events. Sports are also popular for some groups. These include soccer in most countries, kick-boxing in Kyrgyzstan, ice hockey and horse racing in Kazakhstan, and archery and wrestling in Mongolia.

World Heritage Sites

Important cultural features in Central Eurasia are those that are associated with significant historical, political and religious events. A UNESCO World Heritage Site designation relates to the feature's importance to early history as well as recent events. Some of these are

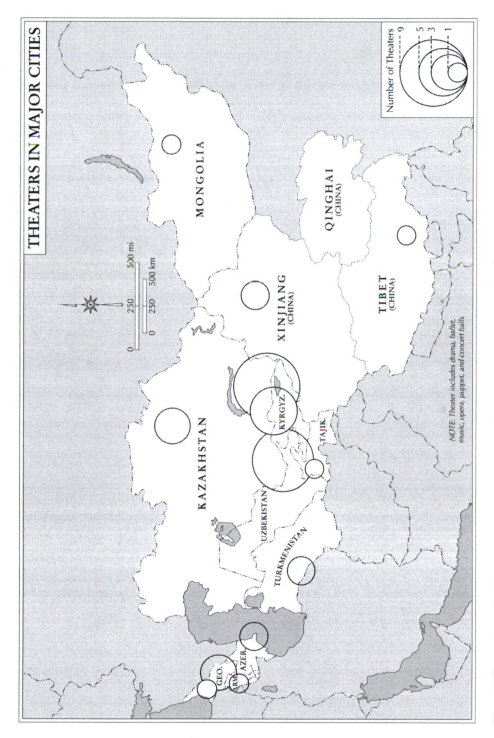

Map 45 Theaters in major cities

WORLD HERITAGE SITES

① Cathedral and Churches of Echmiatsin and the Archaeological Site of Zvartnots
② Monasteries of Haghpat and Sanahin
③ Monastery of Geghard and the Upper Azat Valley
④ Gobustan Rock Art Cultural Landscape
⑤ Walled City of Baku with the Shirvanshah's Palace and Maiden Tower
⑥ Bagrati Cathedral and Gelati Monastery
⑦ Historical Monuments of Mtskheta
⑧ Upper Svaneti
⑨ Mausoleum of Khoja Ahmed Yasawi
⑩ Petroglyphs within the Archaeological Landscape of Tamgaly
⑪ Saryarka – Steppe and Lakes of Northern Kazakhstan
⑫ Sulaiman-Too Sacred Mountain
⑬ Kunya-Urgench
⑭ Parthian Fortresses of Nisa
⑮ State Historical and Cultural Park "Ancient Merv"
⑯ Historic Centre of Bukhara
⑰ Historic Centre of Shakhrisyabz
⑱ Itchan Kala
⑲ Samarkhand – Crossroads of Cultures
⑳ Uvs Nuur Basin
㉑ Orkhon Valley Cultural Landscape
㉒ Historic Ensemble of the Potala Palace, Lhasa

Map 46 World Heritage Sites

archaeological sites; others are major historical mosques, cathedrals and sacred mountains and still other important landmarks of cultural significance. Many of the holy sites are visited by Muslim, Buddhist and Christian supporters who engage in seasonal or annual pilgrimages. These heritage sites are also promoted by many countries on their official websites which are designed to appeal to regional and international tourists. At present there are about thirty World Heritage Sites in Central Eurasia and more than one hundred are on a list to be added in the coming years. These sites are and will become important destinations for future regional and international tourists. Other than the Potala Palace in Lhasa and the Mogao Caves in Dunhuang, Gansu, China has not requested that any cultural or natural sites in western China be listed by UNESCO.

Protected areas

Central Eurasia, because of its unique geographical location in the center of the world's largest land mass, is the home of many unique plants and animals. The importance of protecting this diversity was long recognized during Soviet days with the establishment of national parks and protected areas. Altogether there are several hundred international and national protected nature areas in Central Eurasia. Some are small parks and protected areas and sanctuaries for a unique biological feature; others are large areas (mountains, river valleys, grasslands, forests, etc.) which are rich habitats for unique plants, birds, fish and larger mammals.

Some of these areas are near major populated areas; others are in rather isolated and inaccessible locations far from cities and areas of dense population. Some of these areas are visited by international and national tourists, often with local guides. For the more adventurous

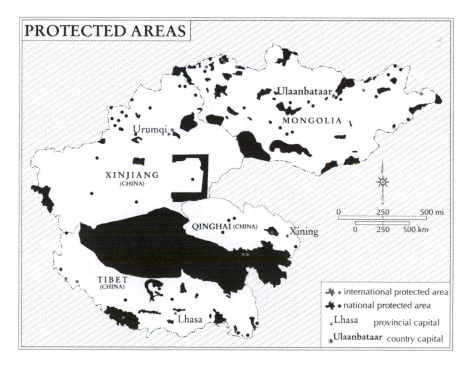

Map 47 Protected areas: Mongolia and west China

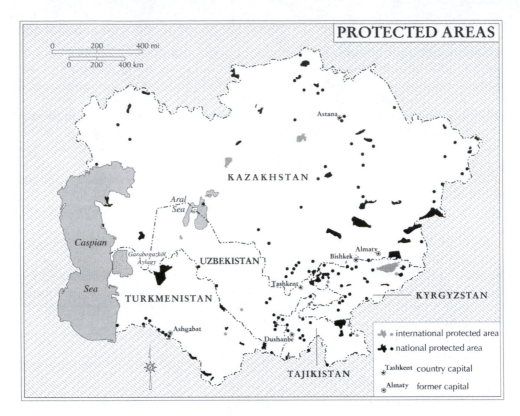

Map 48 Protected areas: Central Asia

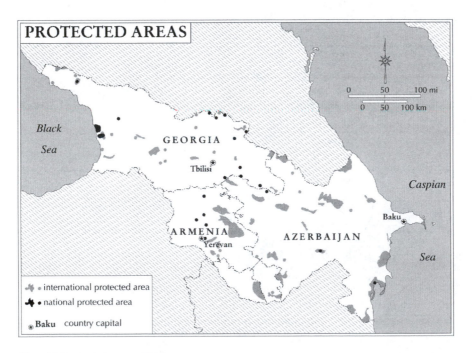

Map 49 Protected areas: Caucasus

hikers and mountain climbers, visiting these places with rare plants and animals as well as spectacular scenery is the purpose of their trip to these states. These will also become important destinations for local, regional and international tourists in the coming years.

Policing and protecting these areas is a problem for many states. International tourists who are also hunters of big game species are among the most difficult to monitor, even if they have official permission to enter a protected area and are accompanied by a local guide. While these protected areas are important bioreserves, they merit the cooperation of local and state officials, scientists and national and international conservation, preservation and environmental organizations.

8   Political

Prison sites and nuclear testing sites

Gulags or secret prisons were major features of the political landscape of the USSR. These were places where dissidents, revolutionaries and others deemed threats to the state were forced to live and work on major projects (roads, railroads, dams, etc.), often in extreme hardship locations. Many prisoners were kept in such places, often for a long time, unknown to their family and friends. During the Cold War it was not uncommon for these gulags, along with military testing stations and weapons factories, not to appear on maps, the thinking being that if these locations were not on maps, they did not exist.

Since the end of the USSR, former prison officials, former prisoners, family members and investigative journalists and social scientists have sought to identify where these gulags were and who was in them. In some cases only crude locations are recorded. What these locations had in common was often their isolation from major population centers, their inaccessibility and remoteness, and also being in places of very harsh environmental conditions.

The accompanying Map 50 shows some located in central Siberia and Central Eurasia (it is impossible to know where all were). The map is likely only partially correct, because there were probably gulags in former republics other than Kazakhstan. Unmarked mass graves and unknown work camps remain part of an unmapped Soviet legacy in many parts of the former Soviet Union.

If one were to overlay the general locations of known and unknown gulags in Kazakhstan with climate, landforms, population density and transportation networks, some reasonable generalizations could be made. They would appear in places, often rural areas, very remote from large cities and regional centers, in extremely harsh environments (very hot in summer, very cold in winter), and very isolated (distant from major railroads, highways and cities). They also might be in some small towns, or simply isolated prison-like settlements distant from any inhabited area. If one flew over these areas today, one might discover abandoned and once-fortified structures on narrow roads distant from nearby towns and cities. Others would be unmarked cemeteries or mass graves, unknown even to locals.

Another secret landscape feature during the time of the Soviet Union was the area of nuclear testing. It was known that the Soviets conducted above and below ground nuclear testing near Semipalatinsk, a heavy industrial city of 300,000 on the Irtysh River in northeast Kazakhstan and near the Soviet border. During nearly five decades the Soviets detonated almost 500 above and below ground nuclear devices. Residents in Semipalatinsk (now called Semey, because the government thinks it "sounds better" and does not have the negative connotation that its previous name does) were about 70 miles (113 km) east of what was termed the Nuclear Polygon. They were only vaguely aware of what was happening

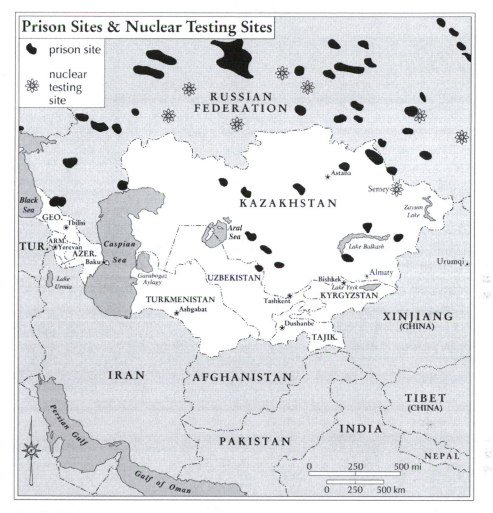

Map 50 Prisons and nuclear testing sites: Central Asia

there; workers were told not to share anything about what they did, but residents did observe the blasts (which were usually unannounced) and felt them (there was often destruction to homes). And many knew that their health problems and those of others (children and elders) were the result of the testing. Within the polygon itself, and at the edge, was a secret city, Kurchatov, which was where the Soviet scientists and families lived, often in extreme luxury compared with the residents of Semipalatinsk. During the Cold War the polygon was surrounded by a barbed wire fence and heavily guarded gates; entry was restricted and so was exit. Today, the border posts are abandoned, the fences are down, and the town has many abandoned buildings alongside the remaining part-derelict buildings. The Kazakh government is establishing a high-tech industrial park in the city. There is also a museum in Kurchatov that is open today for visitors to see the "science" part of the Soviet nuclear testing program. Missing from the displays are photographs of people and people's livelihood being destroyed by the nuclear testing. To see this side of the region's recent history, one has to visit the ethnographic museum in Semey, which provides a rich and pictorial history of the environmental and human damage done by the testing. The city's art museum has no paintings of the nuclear heritage. The city, however, has erected a monument within the past decade to the victims of nuclear testing; this is located in a prominent location in the large public park along the river.

Western China

Details of the prison sites located here are from the Laogai Foundation, Washington, DC. Laogai means reform through labor in Chinese and refers to the vast prison system in China which includes criminals as well as political prisoners. In the prisons, inmates work through the day on farms, factories or mines. James Seymour's 1998 book *New Ghosts, Old Ghosts* cogently discusses the realities of the prison camps (including mines, factories and farms) in Qinghai, Gansu and Xinjiang as documented by the government and by interviews with former inmates of the camps. From Map 51 we see the distribution of the prisons near the larger cities of Lhasa in Tibet, Xining in Qinghai and Urumqi in Xinjiang.

Lop Nur in Xinjiang was the main site for Chinese nuclear weapons testing. China conducted more than forty tests from 1964 till 1996. About half of the tests were above ground. China has not conducted any tests since 1996 after signing (but not yet ratifying) the Comprehensive Nuclear Test Ban Treaty. One Japanese scientist estimates that more than 1.4 million people were affected by fallout and perhaps 190,000 died from diseases related to radiation poisoning. Lop Nur is far from any densely inhabited district, but the fallout from the above ground tests traveled quite a distance.

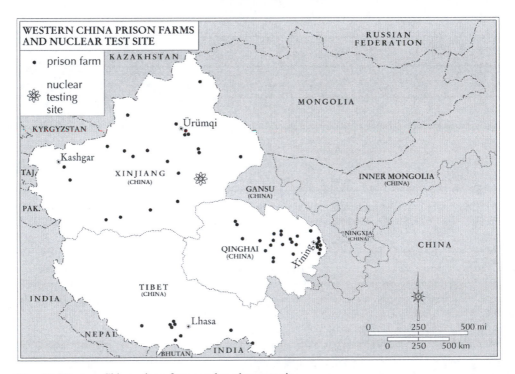

Map 51 Western China prison farms and nuclear test site

Political demonstrations and conflicts

This set of maps highlight political demonstrations and conflict since the 1980s.

West China and Mongolia

In China there were conflicts in 1949–52 as the People's Republic of China (PRC) consolidated its control over western China. Also there were local conflicts during the Cultural Revolution from 1966 to 1969.

Tibet

In general these are Tibetan demonstrations against the PRC. In 1957–59 there were uprisings in Tibet directed against Chinese rule. By 1959 the Dalai Lama had fled Tibet and today he is still in exile in Dharamsala, India. The demonstrations in 1987–89 in Tibet came on the thirtieth anniversary of the 1959 uprising. The March 2008 demonstrations in the Tibetan Autonomous Region, Qinghai and Gansu were timed in part to coincide with the 2008 Olympics in Beijing. Tibetan demonstrations, including self-immolations, continued into 2012 in western Sichuan.

Xinjiang

In general, these are Uyghur demonstrations against the state. In Urumqi, there were political demonstrations but no violence in the late 1980s. By 1990 there was a violent uprising

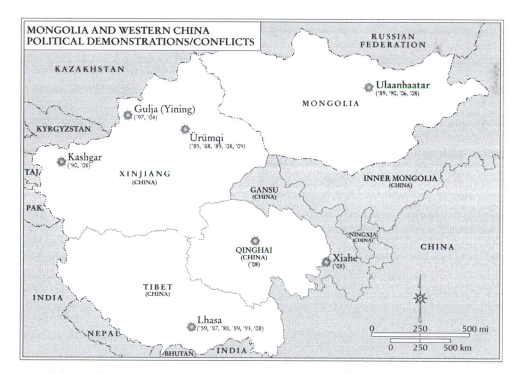

Map 52 Mongolia and western China political demonstrations/conflicts

Map 53 Central Asian political demonstrations/conflicts

just outside Kashgar. In 1997 there was a demonstration, which led to violence in Gulja (Yining). In 2009, Urumqi saw a major demonstration; however, state forces responded aggressively and locals retaliated. It is estimated that some 200 people were killed. In 2011–2012 there were also some disturbances in Kashgar and Hotan.

Mongolia

Ulaanbaatar had protests in 1989, calling for *perestroika* and *glasnost*. In 1990 the demonstrations led to strikes, with the communist government eventually resigning. Free elections were held in July of that year. In 2008 disputes over parliamentary elections again led to protests.

Central Asia

In Central Asia the basis of conflicts came from political changes brought about with the dissolution of the Soviet Union, the transition from authoritarian to democratic rule in the post-Soviet era, and also economic and ethnic tensions.

Tajikistan

Civil war broke out in 1992 with the United Tajik Opposition (composed of liberal reformers and Islamists) against the government forces. Perhaps 100,000 people were killed in this civil war. The conflict continued in a general stalemate from 1993 until 1997 when a peace document was signed by the government and the opposition.

Kyrgyzstan

The Osh riots of 1990 were at the end of the Soviet era and culminated in a clash between Kyrgyz and Uzbek populations. The Tulip Revolution of 2005 resulted in the overthrow of President Akayev, who was seen by many as authoritarian. The 2010 demonstrations in Kyrgyzstan led to the ousting of his replacement, Bakiyev. Uzbek–Kyrgyz clashes continued in Osh though 2010.

Uzbekistan

Islam Karimov has been the leader since 1991. As a strong authoritarian leader, Karimov allows little dissent. One example of dissent, however, was the Andizhan Incident in May 2005 when government forces killed protestors (numbers vary from the official tally of 187 to estimates of between 1,500 and 3,000). Poor economic conditions and government repression in the Fergana Valley contributed to the protest.

Kazakhstan

In 1986 there were protests in Almaty (then Alma-Ata) which spread to other cities over the replacement of a Kazakh party secretary with a Russian party secretary. Today the Kazakhstani government marks this event as the beginning of modern Kazakhstan's struggle for independence. Nursultan Nazarbayev became First Secretary of the Communist Party in Kazakhstan in 1989, assumed office as President of Kazakhstan in 1990, was elected in 1991 as President, and reelected in 1999, 2005 and 2011. The government keeps a tight control on journalists and any opposition. Brief protests and demonstrations broke out in the western cities of Aktau, Zhanaozen and Shetpe in mid-December 2011 with oil workers demanding higher pay.

Turkmenistan

Sapuramat Niyazov (Turkmenbashy) became First Secretary of the Communist Party of the Turkmen SSR in 1985 and then was President of Turkmenistan from 1990 till his death in 2006. His dictatorial rule was marked by caprice, corruption and a cult of personality (for example, he named months after his family, required reading of his book *Ruhnama*, and installed a gold-plated 50 foot tall statue of himself in Ashgabat). The state blamed an assassination attempt in 2002 on opposition leaders. The new president, G. Berdymukhammedov (2007 to present), has moderated his predecessor's policies.

Caucasus

Political conflicts in the Caucasus have been marked by ethnonationalism in the post-Soviet era and by wars between Armenia and Azerbaijan and between Georgia and Russia.

Map 54 Caucasus political demonstrations/conflicts

Georgia

In 1989 the army put down an anti-Soviet demonstration in Tbilisi. The state seceded from the Soviet Union in 1991. In 1992 there was a coup against President Gamsakhurdia. Separatist movements in South Ossetia and Abkhazia resulted in a loss of control over these territories. The Rose Revolution in 2003 forced President Shevardnadze out of office. Demonstrations in 2007 targeted President Saakashvili. Conflicts with Russia in 2006–07 resulted in a war in South Ossetia between joint Russian–Ossetian forces and Georgians in 2008. Russia (and three other states) recognized South Ossetia and Abkhazia as independent in 2008. Georgia, as most other states, does not recognize this independence.

Azerbaijan

In 1989, the Azeri independence movement (Popular Front) organized against the Soviet state. This resulted in Black January 1990, when Soviet troops cracked down on the movement, massacring more than a hundred people in Baku. Heydar Aliyev was leader of Azerbaijan from 1993 to 2003. His son, Ilham Aliyev, has continued his rule (2003 to present). There have been opposition protests, but the Aliyevs have maintained their rule through authoritarian methods. Open warfare between Armenia and Azerbaijan broke out between 1990 and 1994 over Nagorno-Karabakh Republic where the population is mostly Armenian. Since 1994 Nagorno-Karabakh has been internationally recognized as part of Azerbaijan, yet Azerbaijan has no effective control over the area.

Armenia

In 1988 protests against the Soviet Union focused on ecological problems. Armenia was the first non-Baltic state to secede from the Soviet Union in 1990. The 1990–94 conflict between Azerbaijan and Armenia over Nagorno-Karabakh resulted in both Azerbaijan and Turkey closing borders with Armenia, meaning that landlocked Armenia has an open border only with Georgia and to a certain extent Iran. Armenia has experienced protests, but the political system is relatively open. Presidential elections in 2008 generated protests involving thousands of demonstrators in Yerevan.

International organizations

Key international organizations for Central Eurasia include the United Nations, the Organization for Security and Cooperation in Europe, the Commonwealth of Independent States and the Shanghai Cooperation Organization. These international organizations represent the different orientations of the countries. All the countries are members of the UN. The OSCE represents a European group, the CIS represents a post-Soviet group and the SCO represents a Central Eurasian group.

United Nations (UN)

The Republic of China (ROC) was a founding member of the United Nations in 1945 and had a permanent seat on the Security Council. The Republic of China was able to hold up the admission of Mongolia to the UN until 1961. By 1971 the People's Republic of China (PRC) had gained enough influence among member states of the UN for its credentials to be recognized. Since 1971 the PRC rather than the ROC has represented China in the UN.

Table 2 Membership of international organizations

COUNTRY	INTERNATIONAL ORGANIZATIONS			
	OSCE	CIS	SCO	UN
Armenia	1992	1991	na	1992
Azerbaijan	1992	1991	na	1992
Georgia	1992	'91–'08	na	1992
Kazakhstan	1992	1991	1996	1992
Kyrgyzstan	1992	1991	1996	1992
Tajikistan	1992	1991	1996	1992
Turkmenistan	1992	1991	guest	1992
Uzbekistan	1992	1991	2001	1992
Mongolia	na	na	observer	1961
Tibet	na	na	1996	'45,'71
Xinjiang	na	na	1996	'45,'71
Qinghai	na	na	1996	'45,'71

OSCE Organization for Security and Co-operation in Europe
         http://www.osce.org/
CIS   Commonwealth of Independent States
         http://www.cisstat.com/eng/index.htm
SCO   Shanghai Cooperation Organization
         http://www.sectsco.org/EN/
UN   United Nations
         http://www.un.org/en/

The Soviet Union was a founding member of the UN and had a permanent seat on the Security Council. When the Soviet Union split up, new republics formed in 1991. Russia maintained the Permanent Seat on the Security Council in 1991 and the newly formed republics, including Armenia, Azerbaijan, Georgia, Kazakhstan, Kyrgyzstan, Tajikistan, Turkmenistan and Uzbekistan, joined the UN as member states in 1992. UN agencies are at work in Central Eurasia. While all the countries are members of the UN, distinctions do occur. For example, Uzbekistan has not ratified the 1967 Protocol on Refugees, so the UN High Commission on Refugees is hampered in its efforts in that country.

Organization for Security and Cooperation in Europe (OSCE)

The OSCE is a large intergovernmental organization formed initially in 1973 to moderate tensions between East and West in Europe; the USA and USSR were members as well as most European states. The areas of interest for the OSCE include security/military matters, economic development and human rights issues. With the end of the Soviet Union in 1991, the OSCE moved into a new phase and admitted the new republics from the former Soviet Union in 1992. So the Central Eurasian republics have become part of an organization based in Europe. The OSCE is active in Central Eurasia; most notably, Kazakhstan in 2010 held the chairmanship of the organization. OSCE member states regularly send delegations to new states in Eurasia to monitor the transparency of national elections. The United States also sends observer teams.

Commonwealth of Independent States (CIS)

The CIS is a loose association of some of the states of the former Soviet Union. Belarus, Russia and Ukraine first started this association in 1991 to replace the Soviet Union. Central Eurasian states as well as Moldova joined a few weeks later; Armenia, Azerbaijan, Kazakhstan, Kyrgyzstan, Turkmenistan, Tajikistan and Uzbekistan are also members. In 1993, Georgia joined, but in 2008, due to the Russia–Georgia conflict, it left the CIS.

Shanghai Cooperation Organization (SCO)

The SCO is a security organization founded in 1996 by the heads of state of China, Russia, Kazakhstan, Kyrgyzstan and Tajikistan, jointly known as the Shanghai Five. In 2001, Uzbekistan joined the organization, which was then renamed the Shanghai Cooperation Organization. India, Iran, Pakistan and Mongolia have observer status, while the CIS members and Turkmenistan have been guest attendees at meetings.

9   Countries and provinces

Mongolia and west China

Mongolia

The Republic of Mongolia is the second largest landlocked state nestled between Russia, the state with the largest territory, and China, the state with the largest population.

In Mongol Монгол улс (Mongol Uls).

Environment. Much of the environment is steppe, with uplands in the north and west and the Gobi, a desert, in the south. The term *gobi* refers to a rocky semidesert landscape in Mongolian. A *gobi*-style desert should have enough vegetation to support camels. Mountains range as high as Khuiten Peak at 4,374 m (14,346 ft) located in the far western corner of Mongolia at the border with China and Russia. Hot summers and very cold winters characterize the climate.

History. The peak of Mongolian history was during the Mongol empire. In 1206 Genghis Khan unified Mongolia and his sons swept through Asia conquering China, Persia and all the lands in between. Mongol rule over China ended in 1368 and Mongols ruled over their own lands until the Manchu conquest in 1636. The Manchu later ruled Mongolia until 1911. In 1924, the Mongolian People's Republic was formed and followed Communist policy until 1992. After 1992, the Communists morphed into a new political party and the Republic of Mongolia was formed.

Population. Mongolia is the most sparsely populated state in the world. By 2011 estimates, the population numbers around 3 million. Almost half of the population lives in Ulaanbaatar and others in secondary cities such as Darkhan and Erdenet. Urbanization level is 60 percent. The population is young and the total fertility rate is below 2 (which is the replacement rate). More than 90 percent of the population is Mongol, with a minority of Kazakhs in the west.

Culture. Traditional Mongol culture was nomadic, but now more people live in cities. However, in cities there are *ger* alongside apartment blocks. *Ger* are portable homes based on wood lattice and covered in felts. The Mongol language is written using a Cyrillic alphabet. Mongols follow Lama Buddhism; however, the years under Communism resulted in fewer regular Buddhists and a greater secularism in society. Other cultural traditions are still followed including the Naadam or spring festival, with contests of archery, horse racing and wrestling. Modern Mongol culture is thus a combination of city life influenced by globalization including Russian culture, but with roots in nomadism.

Geopolitics. The state is a parliamentary republic with a multiparty system. The largest party, the Mongolian People's Party, was formed out of the former Communist Party in the early 1990s. Mongolia's location between China and Russia has meant that in the

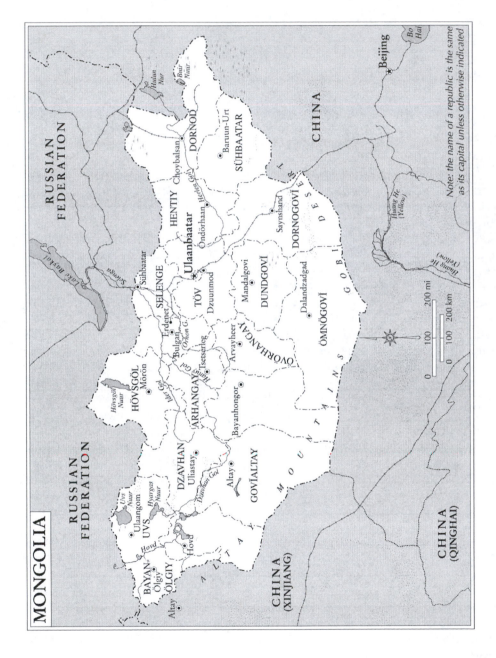

Map 55 Mongolia

Table 3 Mongolia – country facts

Land area	1,566,500 km²
Population	3.13 million
Capital	Ulaanbaatar 949,000
Population density (persons per km²)	2
Predominant religions	Buddhist Lamaist 50%; None 40%
Life expectancy at birth	68.0 yrs.
Under 5 mortality rate (per 1,000)	43
Access to improved water source (%)	76
GNI per capita	$3,330
Area as cropland (%)	n/d
Leading agriculture	Wheat; barley; vegetables; sheep; goats; cattle
Leading industry	Construction; mining; animal products
Merchandise trade (% of GDP)	102.9
Foreign direct investment (% of GDP)	10.8
Internet users (%)	12.2
Carbon dioxide emissions per capita (metric tons)	3.4

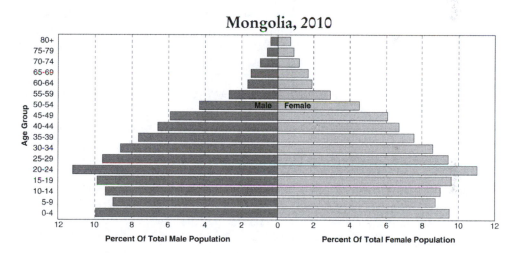

Figure 18 Mongolia, 2010 (population pyramid)

pre-modern era a tension existed between Mongolia and China, and in the modern era (1921–92), Mongolia was a Soviet satellite. Current geopolitical orientations are not necessarily linked with China or Russia but with Japan and the USA.

Development. The economy has traditionally been based on herding and agriculture, with 30 percent of the people being nomadic or seminomadic. After 1992 the country began to have more of a market economy rather than a socialist economy. The current economy favors mineral production from deposits of copper, gold, coal and molybdenum. The major trading partners are China and Russia. Major exports include copper, apparel, livestock, animal products and cashmere. Major imports include machinery, fuel, vehicles and foodstuffs. Life expectancy and mortality rates have improved since the early 1990s, but difficulties remain in the countryside. The population is 97 percent literate.

Western China

Our atlas considers three provincial-level units in China: the Xinjiang Uyghur Autonomous Region, Tibetan Autonomous Region and Qinghai Province. Other areas bordering Central Eurasia include Gansu Province, Inner Mongolia Autonomous Region, Ningxia Hui Autonomous Region, Sichuan and Yunnan. The bulk of the population in these provincial-level units is Han which puts them in the transition zone between Central Eurasia and East Asia.

Tibetan Autonomous Region

The Tibetan Autonomous Region (TAR) was created in 1965 as a provincial-level unit in China; it covers the southern half of the Tibetan Plateau. In cultural/historical Tibet, this area is known as U-Tsang and western Kham. In Tibetan, the name for this land is Bod (Bö). The Chinese name for the Region is Xizang, or Western Tsang.

In Chinese 西藏自治区 (Xizang Zizhiqu).

In Tibetan བོད་རང་སྐྱོང་ལྗོངས་ (Bod-rang–Skyong-ljongs).

Environment. The Tibetan Plateau sits at higher elevations (10,000–14,000 ft, 3,048–4,267 m). Mt Everest (Jomoglangma, Holy Mother), at the southern edge of Tibet on the border with Nepal, is the highest point in the world at 8,848m (29,021 ft). The northern segment of the plateau, called the Chang Tang, is dotted with lakes, while the southern segment has many river systems and valleys. The Indus, Brahmaputra and Salween rivers all have their origins in this part of the plateau. Winters are cold, summers are short

History. Recorded histories date back to the seventh century with the formation of the Tibetan empire which had conflicts with Tang China in the eighth century. Mongols controlled the region from the thirteenth century to the 1330s. Local control continued until the eighteenth century with the advent of the Manchu conquest. The Qing/Manchu allowed political autonomy in the region, where the Dalai Lama was the main authority. After the Qing fell apart, the Dalai Lama ruled Tibet, from 1912 to 1950. In 1951 a seventeen-point agreement between Tibetan authorities and the PRC established Chinese sovereignty in the area. However, many Tibetans rebelled against Chinese control and the Dalai Lama fled to India in 1959, where he resides in exile.

Population. The TAR is the most sparsely populated provincial-level unit in China with almost 3 million people. Much of the population lives in rural settlements. Lhasa is the largest city of over 350,000 and another 100,000 migrants. Much of the population is ethnic Tibetan (almost 95 percent). However, there is a great periodic influx of Han migrants during the spring and summer who work in construction and other projects. In the winter they go back to Sichuan or other parts of China. These are part of the floating population.

Culture. Tibetan culture is very distinct from Chinese. The language is related to Burmese and is written with a Brahmi script derived from Sanskrit. Buddhism, coming from India and Nepal, supplanted the traditional Bon religion. This variant of Mahayana and Vajrayana Buddhism has several traditions including the Gelukpa whose temporal head is the Dalai Lama. Art and architecture connect with India as well. Music, food and customs are more distinctively Tibetan. The major food is *tsampa*, which is roasted barley flour, made into dumplings or noodles. Yak, goat and mutton are the main meats supplemented by yak dairy products.

Geopolitics. A focal issue is the continued exile of the Dalai Lama in India. The Tibetan community in exile in India has formed its own government and elects its own leaders.

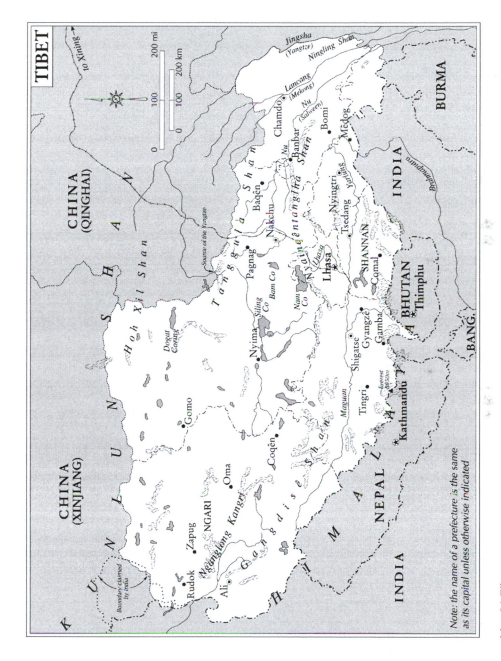

TIBET

CHINA
(QINGHAI)

CHINA
(XINJIANG)

to Xining

0   100   200 mi
0   100   200 km

K U N L U N   S H A N

Hoh Xil Shan

Dogai Coring

Source of the Yangtze

T a n g g u l a   S h a n

Jingsha
(Yangtze)

Ningling Shan

Lancang
(Mekong)

Chamdo

Nu
(Salween)

Nu

Banbar

Bomi

Mêdog

Shan

Ngainqêntanglha

Bagên

Nagqu

Nyainqêntanglha

Nyingtri

Tsedang

yurlung

Gomo

Pagnag

Siling
Co

Bam Co

Nam
Co

Lhasa

Lhasa

SHANNAN

Coqal

INDIA

BURMA

Nyima

Siling

Coqên

Gangdisê Shan

Maquan

Shigatse

Gyangzê

Gamba

BHUTAN
Thimphu

BANG.

Tingri

Everest
8850m

Kathmandu

NEPAL

H I M A L A Y A

INDIA

Oma

NGARI

Zapug

Nganglong Kangri

Rudok

Ali

Boundary claimed
by India

Note: the name of a prefecture is the same
as its capital unless otherwise indicated

Map 56 Tibet

Table 4 Tibet – province facts

Land area	1,202,072 km^2
Population	3.00 million
Capital	Lhasa 373,000
Population density (persons per km^2)	2.0
Predominant religions	Lama Buddhist 95%; Secular/Other 5%
Life expectancy at birth	M 62.5, F 66.2
Under 5 mortality rate (per 1,000)	n/d
Access to improved water source (%)	50–79
GDP per capita	$2,370
Area as cropland (%)	0.2
Leading agriculture	Barley; wheat; sheep; cattle
Leading industry	Food-processing; tourism; mining
Merchandise trade (% of GDP)	n/d
Foreign direct investment (% of GDP)	n/d
Internet users (%)	24.0
Carbon dioxide emissions per capita (metric tons)	n/d

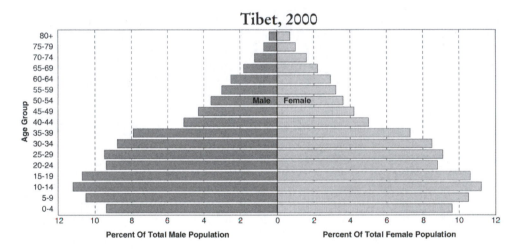

Figure 19 Tibet, 2000 (population pyramid)

The Dalai Lama is now the spiritual head of the community and has stepped down from his political role in the Tibetan government in exile. China has its leaders in the TAR including a party secretary who is Han and a governor who is Tibetan. The regime was particularly brutal during the Cultural Revolution in the 1960s. China adopted more hard-line policies in Tibet after 1987 and demonstrations against China have occurred in Tibet in 1987–89, in 2008, and continue today. Tibet borders India and Nepal. China's relations with India have improved since the border conflicts between the two in the 1960s.

Development. Tibet has the lowest rankings of China's provinces whether in terms of per capita income or the Human Development Index. The educational system is not well developed and most schools in Tibet use Chinese rather than Tibetan as the medium of instruction. The northern areas of the TAR were associated with nomadism and animal raising (yak, sheep, goats) while the south was the site of agricultural crops (barley, buckwheat, potatoes, legumes, mustard). Tourism adds to the economy. China's Western Development Program included the construction of a railway linking the TAR with Qinghai and thus to the rest of the Chinese rail network. Recently, mineral reserves of zinc, copper and lead have been discovered.

Qinghai Province

Qinghai means "blue-green lake" in Chinese and the province is named after the lake in its northeast corner called Köke Naghur in Mongol. The southern area of the province is known as Kham to Tibetans and the eastern area is known as Amdo.

In Chinese 青海省 (Qinghai Sheng).

Environment. Qinghai covers the northern portion of the Tibetan Plateau. The Hoh Xil and Kunlun mountains separate the province into northern and southern sections. The northern part of the province is in the Qaidam Basin (Pendi) which has an elevation of 10,000 ft (3,048 m). This intermontane basin is relatively dry. Qinghai Lake is a very large salt lake. The Yellow (Huang He) and Yangzi (Chang Jiang) rivers both originate in this northern portion of the Tibetan Plateau. The 2010 earthquake in Yushu in the southeast killed several thousand people.

History. Qinghai was a part of the Tibetan Empire. The Kham and Amdo regions were ruled by local authorities and were not necessarily directly controlled by Lhasa. Amdo in particular was on the border between Tibet and China in the ninth century. The Mongols conquered Amdo and Kham in the thirteenth century and began Mongolia's close cultural relationship with Tibet. In the seventeenth century, Ming Chinese, Mongol and Lhasa Tibetans controlled various parts of Amdo and Kham and the Manchu established their control in the following century. After the Qing fell apart in 1912, Amdo and Kham were controlled by local Tibetans and warlords. The Republic of China incorporated Amdo into Qinghai Province in 1928. By 1949–52, Qinghai was controlled by the People's Republic.

Population. The population is about 5–6 million. Ethnic groups include Han, Tibetan, Hui, Tu (Mongour), Salar and Mongols. Just over half are Han. Xining (population approximately 1.2 million) is the capital and major center (Xining means "west pacify" in Chinese).

Culture. Besides Han and Tibetans, other groups include the Hui, Salar, Tu and Mongol. The Hui are Sino-Muslim, the Salar are Muslims who speak a Turkic language, and the Tu follow a combination of Confucianism and Buddhism and speak a Mongolic language. There are large Tibetan monasteries as well as mosques and temples. While Xining has a developed city culture, much of the province is still rural in nature.

Geopolitics. Qinghai is well known for having a large number of *laogai* or work-reform prison camps which house political prisoners as well as criminals. Dissidents such as Wei Jingsheng were imprisoned in Qinghai laogai. The Dalai Lama was born in Amdo in this province. Demonstrations against the state have occurred in Qinghai as well as Tibet. Other than Xining and Haidong prefecture, all of the other prefectures are Tibetan and Mongol autonomous prefectures, meaning that Tibetan and Mongol languages are used.

Development. The traditional economy was pastoral and agricultural, including rapeseed and wheat. The Qaidam Basin has vast mineral reserves including lithium, magnesium and sodium as well as asbestos, borax, oil and salt. Laogai prisoners work in the mines. Before the economic development programs of the 1980s and 1990s, laogai contributed a major portion of the Qinghai economy. Xining has factories which process the minerals and chemicals, with rail linkages to Gansu since 1959 and on to Lhasa since 2006.

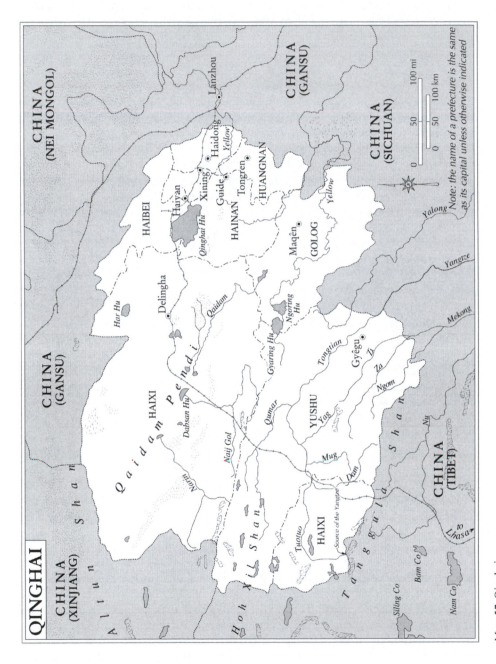

Map 57 Qinghai

Table 5 Qinghai – province facts

Land area	717,481 km^2
Population	5.63 million
Capital	Xining 1,198,304
Population density (persons per km^2)	8
Predominant religions	Secular/Other 58%; Lama Buddhist 24%; Muslim 18%
Life expectancy at birth	M 64.6, F 67.7
Under 5 mortality rate (per 1,000)	n/d
Access to improved water source (%)	50–79
GDP per capita	$3,038
Area as cropland (%)	0.7
Leading agriculture	rapeseed; wheat; sheep
Leading industry	salt; chemicals; minerals
Merchandise trade (% of GDP)	n/d
Foreign direct investment (% of GDP)	n/d
Internet users (%)	7.0
Carbon dioxide emissions per capita (metric tons)	4–5

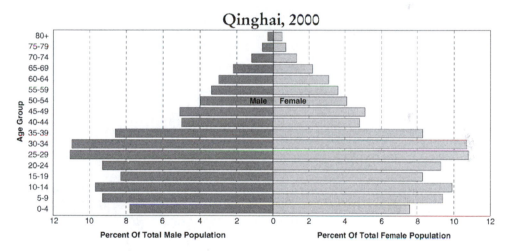

Figure 20 Qinghai, 2000 (population pyramid)

Historic or cultural Tibet

Historic or cultural Tibet has three cultural regions – U-Tsang in the southwest, Kham in the southeast and Amdo in the north. Tibetan populations still live in these regions. Under the administration of the People's Republic of China, U-Tsang is mostly in the Tibetan Autonomous Region (TAR), Kham is in eastern TAR, Sichuan and Yunnan provinces, while Amdo is in Qinghai and Gansu provinces. China has Tibetan autonomous prefectures in Qinghai, southwest Gansu, western Sichuan and northwest Yunnan. Most of these regions are a part of the Tibetan Plateau. Tibetan cultural influences extend to Bhutan, Nepal, and

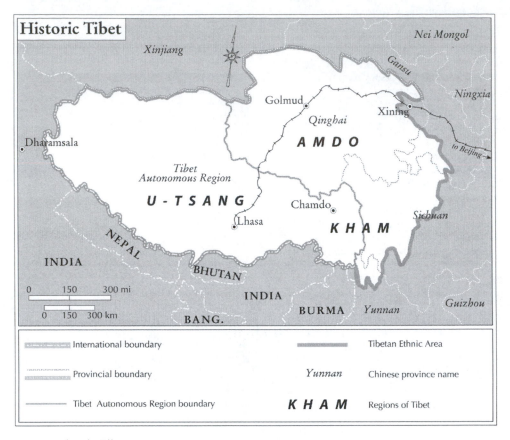

Map 58 Historic Tibet

regions of India such as Sikkim and Ladakh. The Dalai Lama is in exile in Dharamsala in India.

Amdo. This region is mostly agricultural and pastoral. Today eastern Amdo and Xining are mostly Han while the rest is mostly Tibetan. By the mid-eighteenth century much of Amdo was not ruled directly from Lhasa. Many Tibetan Lamas including the current fourteenth Dalai Lama and the tenth Panchen Lama are from this area. The Labrang monastery in Gansu is one of the most important religious centers in Amdo.

Kham. This region has rugged terrain caused by the river valleys of the Yangtze, Mekong, Salween and Yarlung rivers. The Tibetans here are known as Khampa. In the eighteenth century eastern Kham was included into provinces administered by the Manchu Qing separately from Lhasa. Kham people are pastoralists and agriculturalists today.

U-Tsang. This region is southwestern Tibet, mostly in the TAR. Tsang refers to the western segment while U is the center around Lhasa. The northern parts of U-Tsang are plateau with mostly nomadic pastoralists, while the southern parts of U-Tsang are the agriculture area with its river valleys such as that of the Yarlung. Lhasa with its important cultural sites of the Potala Palace and Jokhang Temple is located in U-Tsang.

Xinjiang Uyghur Autonomous Region

This is the largest provincial level unit in China (just a bit larger than Mongolia). The Chinese called the area "Xiyu" (Western regions) until the 1880s. The general term in English for the area is Eastern Turkestan as opposed to Western Turkestan (east and west of Kashgar). The term Xinjiang means "new frontier" in Mandarin and comes from the Qing Manchu designation of the area in the 1880s when it became a province.

In Chinese 新疆维吾尔自治区 (Xinjiang Weiwuer Zizhiqu).

In Uyghur Shinjang Uyghur Aptonom Rayoni

Environment. Xinjiang is mostly desert, with oases and mountains. The elevations range from Mt. K-2 (locally known as Khogir) in the Karakoram Range at 8,611 m (28,251 ft) down to the Turpan Depression at –155 m (469 ft) below sea level. Thus Xinjiang has the second highest and second lowest point on earth. The province is divided north and south

Map 59 Xinjiang

Table 6 Xinjiang – province facts

Land area	1,664,897 km^2
Population	21.81 million
Capital	Urumqi 2,300,000
Population density (persons per km^2)	13
Predominant religions	Muslim 59%; Secular/Other 41%
Life expectancy at birth	66 yrs.
Under 5 mortality rate (per 1,000)	n/d
Access to improved water source (%)	50–79
GDP per capita	$3,038
Area as cropland (%)	0.2
Leading agriculture	Cotton; fruits
Leading industry	natural gas, crude oil
Merchandise trade (% of GDP)	n/d
Foreign direct investment (% of GDP)	7.6
Internet users (%)	6.0
Carbon dioxide emissions per capita (metric tons)	4–5

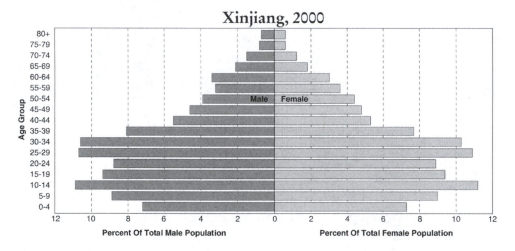

Figure 21 Xinjiang, 2000 (population pyramid)

by the Tian Shan (Heavenly Mountain) Range. The Tarim Basin (Pendi) occupies most of southern Xinjiang; the Junggar Basin (Pendi) is the largest physical unit in the north. The Ili River forms a well-watered segment north of the Tian Shan. In the middle of the Tarim Basin is the Taklamakan, a huge desert tract of shifting sands. The Tarim and the Ili are both rivers of interior drainage. In Turpan, traditional underground canals known as *karez* (*qanat*) irrigate the land.

History. The region has long been an important segment of the Silk Road. Its long history begins with a variety of Indo-European peoples variously known as Saka, Tokharian or Yuezhi. Han Chinese first came into the area during the Han Dynasty. Groups of Turkic peoples and other Central Asian nomads migrated into the area and intermarried with the

Indo-Europeans. Han came again into the area in the eighth and ninth centuries. Chinese imperial control faltered in the region between 750 and 1750. During this time, at first Uyghur, then Mongol followed by Chagatai and then the Khojas (Turkic Islamic leaders) held control. The Manchu conquered the region, adding it to the Qing Empire. After the Qing, warlords held sway in Xinjiang during the Republic of China. In the 1930s there was an East Turkestan Islamic Republic in Kashgar and in the 1940s an East Turkestan republic in Gulja (Yining). The People's Republic controlled the region by 1949 and Kashgar by 1952.

Population. Xinjiang has nearly 22 million people. Urumqi (Ürümchi, Wulumuqi) is the largest city and capital of the region. Kashgar (Kashi), Gulja (Yining), Korla (Kuerle) and Shihezi are secondary cities. Uyghur (Weiwuer) are the most common ethnic group and are concentrated in the south around Kashgar. Han are the next largest group and are concentrated in Urumqi, Shihezi and other cities. Kazakh are the next largest group and are located mostly in the north around Altay (Aertai). More Han are migrating from other parts of China, with the result that in a few years Han may become not just a plurality but a majority.

Culture. Mandarin and Uyghur are both used in Xinjiang. A bilingual landscape has developed for everything from the names of cities and other places to cultural identities. With the addition of the Kazakh, Hui, Kyrgyz and Mongol minorities, Xinjiang has a complex cultural landscape as diverse as the physical landscape. Uyghur, Kazakh and Kyrgyz are all Muslim and Turkic; thus the cultural base is very different from that of the Han. The Hui are between the Han and the Turkic peoples of Xinjiang as they are Muslim but speak Chinese. Uyghur food includes *nan* (bread) baked in a *tonur* (tandoori) oven, *leghmen* (hand-pulled noodles) or *pollao* (a rice pilaf). So the cultural landscape is divided by language, religion, food, music and customs.

Geopolitics. The Xinjiang Uyghur Autonomous Region was formed out of Xinjiang Province in 1955. In autonomous regions in China, minority populations are allowed the use of their language and religion and to follow their customs. The state does not allow or tolerate expressions of independence from the PRC. Since the 1990s, there have been a number of political disturbances, some of which have become violent. Xinjiang is on China's border with Pakistan, Afghanistan, Tajikistan, Kyrgyzstan, Kazakhstan, Russia and Mongolia. China's relations with all these countries hinge upon security issues in Xinjiang.

Development. While Xinjiang does not have a lot of water, the region does have oil and cotton. These two products have now formed the backbone of the economy. Xinjiang's petrochemical economy delivers a higher per capita gross domestic product than much of western China (though nowhere near that of eastern China). The oil comes from fields in the middle of the Tarim and in the north at Karamay. However, the bulk of the population have not benefited from this petrochemical economy. Oil is controlled by the state. Another sector of the economy is agriculture, producing cotton and fruits in irrigated lands. The Xinjiang Production and Construction Corps controls much of the good land and many factories in the region; this control is a holdover from previous state farm systems. In general the Uyghur live in poorer conditions than the Han in the region. New railroads, airports and roads link Xinjiang to the rest of China and are part of China's Western Development Program begun in 1999.

The Tarim Basin

The Tarim Basin is a large basin of interior drainage covering some 900,000 km^2 (347,400 sq. mi) in southern Xijiang.

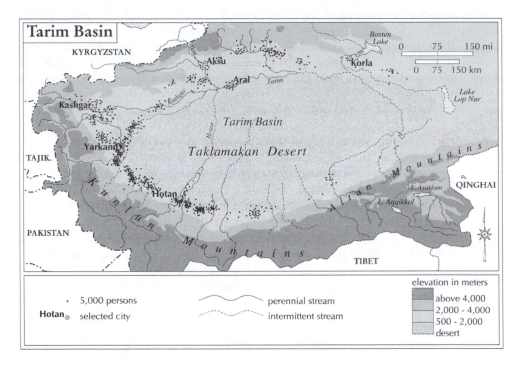

Map 60 Tarim Basin

Environment. The Tarim River is formed by the confluence of the Kashgar, Yarkand and Hotan rivers flowing north out of the Kunlun and Karakoram mountains. The Tarim River formerly flowed into Lop Nur (Lop Lake), but the water from the river is mostly used up by irrigation and evaporation. The interior of the Tarim Basin is occupied by the Taklamakan Desert, which, after the Sahara, is the world's second largest sand dune desert. Due to continentality effects, the desert is very dry but winter nights are very cold. The larger oases are in Kashgar and Hotan.

History. Historically this basin was known as Alte Sheher (Six Cities) or simply Kashgaria, after the main settlement of Kashgar. East out of Kashgar, the Silk Road took a southern and a northern route. The southern route went to Hotan and lay between the Kunlun and the Taklamakan. The northern route followed the oases north of the Taklamakan and south of the Tian Shan range through Aksu and to Korla. These routes converged together in Dunhuang (modern Gansu Province). This region saw independent kingdoms of Indo-European peoples such as the Saka or Tokharian. Xiong-nu and then Turkic people moved into the Tarim, from 100 BCE to 700 CE intermingling with Tokharians. Over the centuries Turks, Uyghurs, Mongols, Manchu and Han ruled the basin. China extended control over the basin during the Han (125 BCE–220 CE), Tang 640–750 and Manchu Qing (1750–1820, 1870–1911) dynasties and reestablished control in 1950–52.

Population and culture. Today the bulk of the population in the Tarim Basin is Uyghur. Han settlements are more pronounced among the cities of Korla, Aksu and Aral. Uyghur settlement is also focused in the Kashgar, Yarkand and Hotan oases. A greater influx of Han migration moved gradually south and west in the latter half of the twentieth century from Korla to Aksu and now to Kashgar. Much of Kashgar's traditional city is being remade into new apartment blocks. Kashgar Prefecture has 4 million residents, Hotan Prefecture 2 million, Aksu Prefecture 2–3 million and Bayangol Mongol Autonomous Prefecture (centered around Korla) 2 million, for a total of about 10–11 million.

Economy. The people of the oases of Kashgar and Hotan engaged in the production of fruit, cotton, wheat and rice for centuries, trading with Central Asia and India along the Silk Road. Korla is the largest industrial center in the basin today (second after Urumqi in all of Xinjiang). Another element in the agricultural and industrial geography is the Xinjiang Production and Construction Corps (XPCC). Composed of demobilized military, the XPCC dominates production in Xinjiang. Aral and centers near Kashgar are totally composed of XPCC members who are mostly Han. The final element of production is oil, production of which in the Tarim accounts for 20 percent of China's total production. To access the oil in the middle of the Taklamakan, China has built new roads and pipelines. The railroad from Korla was extended to Kashgar in 1999 and the Kashgar to Hotan link was completed in 2011.

Central Asia

The traditional name in English for this area is Western Turkestan. The Russians referred to the region as Central Asia and Kazakhstan, as the four southern republics were colonized later than Kazakhstan.

Kazakhstan

The Republic of Kazakhstan is the largest landlocked country in the world and the largest country in Central Eurasia. Kazakhstan means "land of the Kazakhs". Kazakh means independent or free. All of Western Europe could fit in Kazakhstan.

In Kazakh Қазақстан Республикасы (Qazaqstan Respublikasi).

Environment. The northern areas are steppe lands. The southeastern areas include parts of the Tian Shan Range. The northeastern areas include parts of the Altai Mountains and the southwestern areas include the Turan Lowland. Western Kazakhstan borders the Caspian Sea and the Aral Sea. The Syr Darya flows out of Kyrgyzstan and through Kazakhstan into the northern lobe of the Aral Sea. The Ural River flows out of Russia into the Caspian. The Ili River flows out of Xinjiang and to Lake Balkhash. The Ertis (Irtysh) flows out of China, through Kazakhstan and into the Ob in Siberia. Most of the country's hydrography is interior drainage.

History. Indo-Europeans such as the Saka populated the area in prehistory. Turkic peoples settled the area by the sixth century. The Karluk Turks had a state here in the eighth century, by which time Arabs had introduced Islam into the region. The Kharakhanid Turks controlled the southern portions from the ninth to the twelfth century when Mongols moved into the region. After the Mongol Empire in the thirteenth century, the Golden Horde was ruled by Mongols and many people were Kazakhs. The Kazakh Khanate from 1464 to 1731 established rule that was centered between Lake Balkhash and the Tian Shan, the *jetisu*, or Seven Rivers area. Russian rule came in 1731, gradually moving southward. By the mid-nineteenth century much of the territory was under Russian control. The Soviet Union controlled the area as the Kazakh Soviet Socialist Republic from 1917 to 1991.

Population. The country has 15 million people including the major city of Almaty (1.4 million) and the new capital Astana (650,000 in 2009). Almaty means "full of apples" in Kazakh, while Astana means "capital". Kazakhstan has a low population growth rate

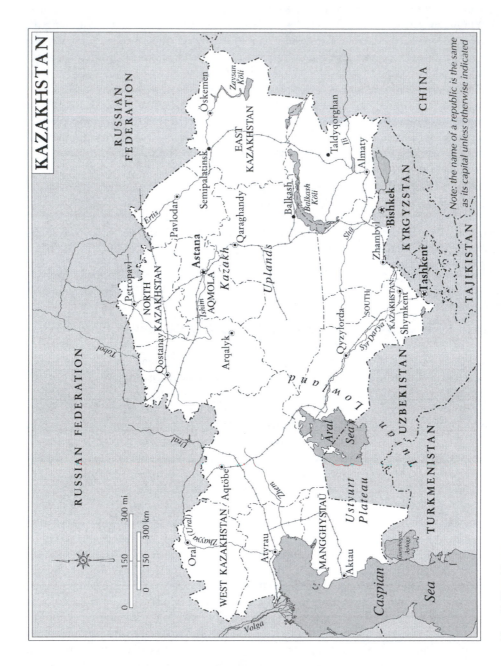

Map 61 Kazakhstan

Table 7 Kazakhstan – country facts

Land area	2,724,900 km²
Population	15.52 million
Capital	Astana 650,000
Largest city	Almaty 1,383,000
Population density (persons per km²)	6
Predominant religions	Muslim 47%; Russian Orthodox 44%
Life expectancy at birth	68.0 yrs.
Under 5 mortality rate (per 1,000)	29
Access to improved water source (%)	96
GNI per capita	$10,320
Area as cropland (%)	11.1
Leading agriculture	grain (mostly spring wheat); cotton; livestock
Leading industry	oil; gas; aluminum
Merchandise trade (% of GDP)	76.5
Foreign direct investment (% of GDP)	7.6
Internet users (%)	12.3
Carbon dioxide emissions per capita (metric tons)	13.3

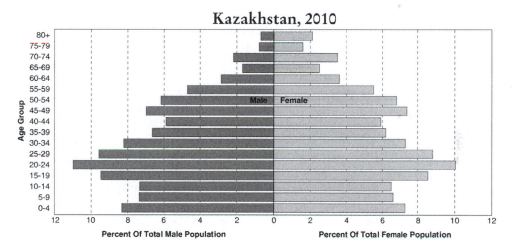

Figure 22 Kazakhstan, 2010 (population pyramid)

and the life expectancy rate is moderate. The urbanization level is 60 percent. Kazakhstan has a large Kazakh population and a significant Russian minority. The proportion of Russians is much higher in Kazakhstan than elsewhere among Central Asian states.

Culture. Kazakhs speak a Turkic language and use a Cyrillic script. Many urban Kazakhs speak Russian and in some cases very little Kazakh. Many Russians and Germans migrated out of Kazakhstan in the 1990s, but substantial numbers remain. Most Kazakhs are Sunni Muslim, while most Russians are Orthodox. The state is secular. Most Russians live in the north or in the Almaty area. Kazakhs were traditionally steppe nomads so traditional foods include mutton, beef or horse and *koumiss* (*kymyz*, fermented horse milk).

Geopolitics. Kazakhstan is a republic, but the president wields much of the power. President Nursultan Nazarbayev has been the leader of the republic since 1991, having previously been First Secretary of the Communist Party of the Kazakh SSR. There are various political parties but the Nur-Otan Party led by Nazarbayev has remained in control. The state moved the capital from Almaty to Astana in 1997. Along with China and Russia, it was a founding member of the Shanghai Cooperation Organization and it chaired the OSCE in 2010. Kazakhstan has the strongest military of the Central Asian states. Nuclear weapons tests were first conducted in Kazakhstan in 1949 by the Soviets, but the state disarmed its nuclear weapons in 1995. Kazakhstan retains the Baikonur Cosmodrome which it rents to the Russians for space flights.

Development. Kazakhstan's economy is larger than all of the other Central Asian states put together. Literacy and education levels are high. Kazakhstan has enormous reserves of oil and gas as well as uranium, copper and zinc. Extractive industries have led to strong economic growth and have set Kazakhstan as the leader in per capita GDP in Central Asia ($12,700 in 2010). Transportation linkages such as rail and pipelines link the country to Russia and China. Kazakhstan is seeking to diversify its economy from the extractive industries into transport, chemicals and telecommunications. Major agricultural products include wheat and cotton from the steppe. China and Russia are the major trading partners.

Kyrgyzstan

Officially known as the Kyrgyz Republic, it lies between Kazakhstan, China, Tajikistan and Uzbekistan. Kyrgyzstan has seen the ouster of two presidents since the founding of the country after the dissolution of the Soviet Union in 1991. Kyrgyz means "forty" and refers to an ancestor origin myth.

In Кыргуз Кыргыз Республикасы (Kyrgyz Respublikasi).

Environment. Kyrgyzstan is farther from the ocean than any other country in the world. Mountains of the Tian Shan Range cover most of the country. Ysyk Köl (Issyk Kul, Hot Lake) in the north is the second largest alpine lake in the world. Most rivers flow westward and form the Syr Darya in Uzbekistan. Kyrgyzstan has an advantage as an upstream user and has hydroelectric potential. Much of the country has highland climates, but the Fergana Valley, which is shared with Uzbekistan, is much warmer and quite hot in summer. Many of the mountains are covered in forest up to the tree line.

History. Indo-European tribes such as Saka (Scythians) settled in the area in prehistory. Kyrgyz and other Turkic peoples migrated into the area by the seventh century, with the Kharakhanid Turks controlling southern portions from the ninth to the twelfth century, centered on Balasaghun near Bishkek. Kyrgyz nomads lived in the Tian Shan Range through 1200 and were eventually conquered by the Mongols. Kyrgyz lived in areas controlled by the Mongol Chagatai as well as the Golden Horde. Warfare with Mongols, Chinese and Manchus was constant in Kyrgyz history. This was also the time of Manas, the hero of the Kyrgyz national epic. By the late nineteenth century, Russia had absorbed the Kyrgyz into its empire. From 1919 to 1991, Soviet control was established in the Kyrgyz Soviet Socialist Republic.

Population. Kyrgyzstan has a population of 5–6 million. The population growth rate is 1.4 percent. Much of the population is rural with an urbanization rate of 35 percent. Kyrgyz account for 65 percent of the population, with Uzbeks also comprising a significant component, especially in the Fergana Valley. Bishkek, the capital, has a population of 850,000 and is located in the north. Osh, in the Fergana Valley, is the second largest city at 200,000 inhabitants.

Map 62 Kyrgyzstan

Table 8 Kyrgyzstan: country facts

Land area	199,900 km^2
Population	5.5 million
Capital	Bishkek 854,000
Population density (persons per km^2)	27
Predominant religions	Muslim 75%; Russian Orthodox 20%
Life expectancy at birth	70.0 yrs.
Under 5 mortality rate (per 1,000)	41
Access to improved water source (%)	89
GNI per capita	$2,200
Area as cropland (%)	0.38
Leading agriculture	Tobacco; cotton; potatoes; sheep; wool
Leading industry	Machinery; textiles; food-processing
Merchandise trade (% of GDP)	102.2
Foreign direct investment (% of GDP)	6.5
Internet users (%)	14.3
Carbon dioxide emissions per capita (metric tons)	1.1

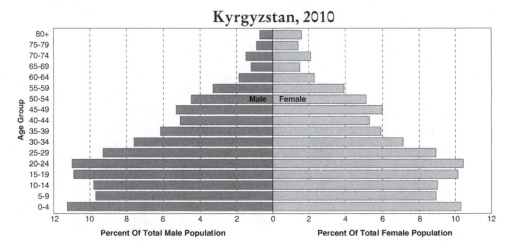

Figure 23 Kyrgyzstan, 2010 (population pyramid)

Culture. The Kyrgyz speak a Turkic language and use a Cyrillic script, and they were traditionally nomads living in the mountain areas. Traditional foods included horsemeat, mutton and *koumiss* (fermented mares' milk). Traditionally people lived in portable felt structures (in Russian and English, *yurt*). The Kyrgyz are Muslim, but as many were nomadic, there were few mosques, rather people worshipped at home. The Uzbeks in the south are also Turkic and Muslim and have their mosques in the villages where they are settled. Russian is a common language in the city. Many Russians and Germans emigrated out of Kyrgyzstan in the 1990s seeking work.

Geopolitics. Kyrgyzstan has actually expelled authoritarian leaders: in 2005 Akayev was ousted during the Tulip Revolution and in 2010 Bakiyev was expelled. After Roza Otunbayeva was an interim president, Almazbek Atambayev was elected President in

December 2011. Since the formation of the state in 1991, tensions with Uzbekistan have revolved around the border but also use of water from the Syr Darya. There are a number of Uzbek enclaves in southern Kyrgyzstan and in 2010 there were riots in Osh, which developed into Kyrgyz–Uzbek ethnic conflicts. In terms of foreign relations, Kyrgyzstan is on good terms with Russia and Kazakhstan and is a member of the Shanghai Cooperation Organization. Kyrgyzstan also leases the Manas Transit Center to the USA to conduct refueling for jets going to Afghanistan.

Development. Kyrgyzstan has a low per capita GDP ($2,200). Much of the local economy is focused on crops and animals. Exports include gold and mercury as well as cotton, wool and meat. China, Russia, Uzbekistan and Kazakhstan are important trade partners. Potentials include hydroelectric power and tourism. Vast tracts of mountains and pastures attract sport tourism based on mountaineering and riding horses. Literacy levels are high. A big component of the economic sector is foreign aid and NGOs.

The Fergana Valley

The Fergana Valley is a large (22,000 km^2 or 7,920 sq. mi) valley which is divided between Uzbekistan, Tajikistan and Kyrgyzstan. Political, environmental, cultural, demographic and economic geographies combine to make this a critical crossroads location in Central Eurasia.

Environment. The Naryn and Kara-Kul'dzha rivers flow west out of the Fergana and Chatkal Mountains in Kyrgyzstan and join near Namangan to form the Syr Darya. The Syr exits west out of the valley on to Tajikistan and then back into Uzbekistan. The Fergana Valley is relatively well-watered with fertile soil compared with the surrounding deserts to the west. With global climate change the valley will get warmer, glaciers will melt and the summer flow of water into the Syr Darya will be lessened. Earthquakes are also common in the area.

History. Because of the fertile soil in the area, the valley attracted many settlers. The Chinese Han Dynasty spoke of this region as Da Yuan as far back as 120 BCE. Indo-European people settled along this major artery of the Silk Road. Turkic peoples, Arabs and Persians held sway. The Mongols and then Timur added the valley to their conquests. Babur, the founder of the Mughal Empire in India, came from Fergana. By the late 1800s Fergana was a part of Russian Turkestan. In the 1920s, portions of the valley were attached to the Uzbek, Kyrgyz and Tajik SSRs.

Geopolitics. When the valley was in one country, the Soviet Union, there was not too much confusion. However, 1989/90 brought conflict. The Soviet division of the valley presaged a number of geopolitical issues with independence in 1991. All three countries claim their territorial spaces across the valley floor. Uzbekistan has several exclaves surrounded by Kyrgyzstan. The natural exit of the valley proceeds westward through Tajikistan. So the connections from Tashkent to Fergana are made difficult. One must either go through Tajikistan (which is where the railroad lies) or over the mountain roads and through tunnels. In addition, Uzbekistan periodically closes the border limiting trade in the valley. Refugees on both sides of the Uzbek/Kyrgyz border derive from unrest in Andizhan in 2005 and in Jalal-Abad and Osh in 2010.

Demography and culture. This is the most densely populated segment of Central Asia. There are more than 10 million people in the valley, including 1.8 million in Kyrgyzstan (Osh and Jalal-Abad), 2 million in Tajikistan (Khujand) and 6.5 million in Uzbekistan (Andizhan or Andijan, Namangan, Kokand, and the city of Fergana). Uzbek, Kyrgyz and Tajik ethnicities are common and intermingle in the valley. Most of the Uzbeks in Kyrgyzstan

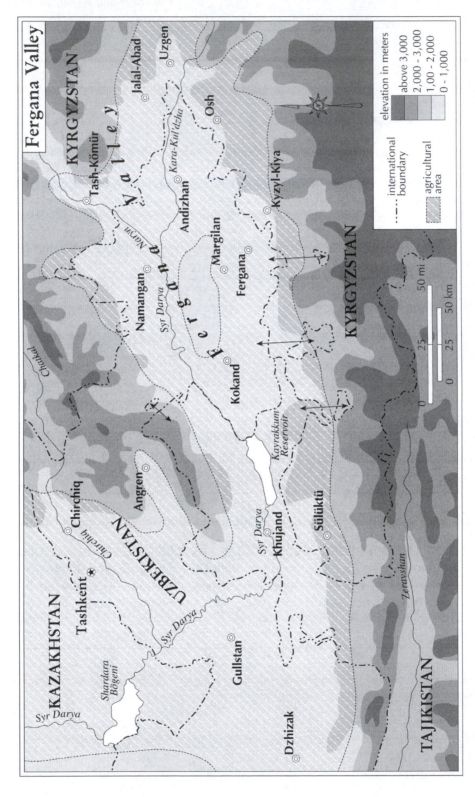

Map 63 Fergana Valley

reside here, together with most of the Kyrgyz in Uzbekistan and most of the Uzbeks in Tajikistan.

Economy. In ancient times, cotton, horses and silk were the main products in the area. Today, cotton fields, mulberry trees (for the silkworms), orchards and vineyards cover the valley in a dense agricultural landscape. Deposits of oil, natural gas and iron ore appear on the edges of the valley floor. Industrial activities include the Daewoo joint venture automobile plant near Andizhan and also food-processing, chemicals, cement, cotton milling, and still some silk weaving.

Tajikistan

The Republic of Tajikistan borders Kyrgyzstan, China, Afghanistan and Uzbekistan. Tajik comes from a Turk word for Iranian speakers. Tajikistan is the only Central Asian state where Turkic people are not a majority. It is the smallest of the Central Asian states.

In Tajik Ҷумхурии Тоҷикистон (Çumhuriji Toçikiston).

Environment. Tajikistan is a very mountainous country. The eastern half is in the Pamir. Ismoil Somoni Peak near the center of the country reaches a height of 7,495 m. The Syr Darya flows through the Fergana Valley in the northern segment. The Panj (which forms the border with Afghanistan), Vakhsh and Kafirnigan rivers are tributaries to the Amu Darya. The physiography is very rugged. While the Fergana Valley and Dushanbe are warm, the mountainous Pamir region has cold highland climates.

History. Indo-European peoples such as Scythians (Saka) lived in the area in prehistory. The area was in Bactria and Sogdiana and was ruled successively by the Greeks, Kushan and Hephthalite empires from *c.*300 BCE to 550 CE. Arabs brought Islam and ruled from *c.*700 to 850 CE. Today, Tajikistan identifies with the Persian Samanid Dynasty which ruled from *c.*900 to 1000. The Turks, Mongols and Timurids ruled 1000–1740, then the Persians, followed by the Russians from 1868. From 1920 to 1991 the area was the Tajik Soviet Socialist Republic in the Soviet Union.

Population. Estimates show Tajikistan to have a population of about 7 million. The population growth rate is 1.8 percent and the urbanization rate is low at 26 percent. Dushanbe, the capital, is the largest city at 700,000 inhabitants, with Khujand in Fergana the second largest at 150,000. Tajiks account for 80 percent of the population with Uzbeks accounting for another 15 percent.

Culture. Tajiks use a Cyrillic script to write their language which is a variant of Farsi or Persian. There are many Russian loanwords. Uzbeks speak a Turkic language also written in Cyrillic. Tajikistan may move to a Perso-Arabic alphabet. The most common religion is Islam, with Sunni being the dominant variety rather than Shi'a. Many Russians left during the civil war in the 1990s. While Russian is commonly used, it is no longer the official language. There are more Tajiks in Afghanistan than in Tajikistan. A traditional dish is *palav*, a rice pilaf, and green tea.

Geopolitics. After independence in 1991, Tajikistan fought a civil war from 1992 to 1997 between the government and the United Tajik Opposition. While the country today is a republic, one party, the People's Democratic Party, has remained in power, with President Rahmon having been the leader since 1992. Tajikistan has good relations with Russia, the USA, China and Afghanistan. Relations with Uzbekistan are a bit testy. Tajikistan is in the Shanghai Cooperation Organization.

Development. Tajikistan remains the poorest of the former Soviet states, with a per capita GDP of $2,000. Many men work abroad in CIS countries to earn remittances to send home.

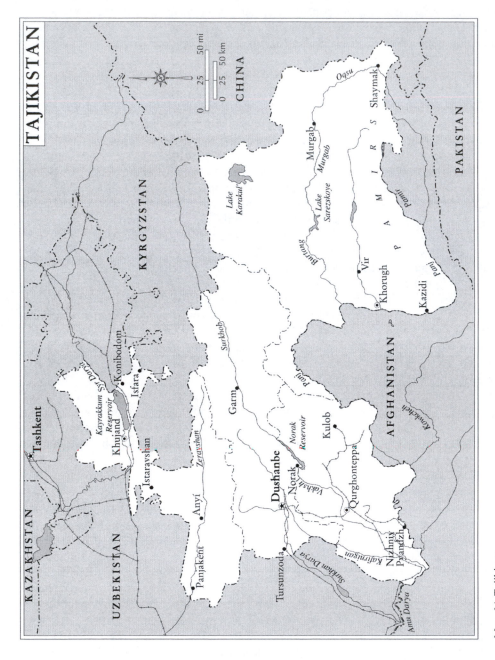

Map 64 Tajikistan

Table 9 Tajikistan – country facts

Land area	142,550 km²
Population	7.63 million
Capital	Dushanbe 704,000
Population density (persons per km²)	47
Predominant religions	Sunni Muslim 85%; Shi'a Muslim 5%
Life expectancy at birth	66.0 yrs.
Under 5 mortality rate (per 1,000)	68
Access to improved water source (%)	70
GNI per capita	$1,950
Area as cropland (%)	0.91
Leading agriculture	Cotton; wheat; fruit
Leading industry	Aluminum; cement
Merchandise trade (% of GDP)	105.7
Foreign direct investment (% of GDP)	12.0
Internet users (%)	0.3
Carbon dioxide emissions per capita (metric tons)	0.8

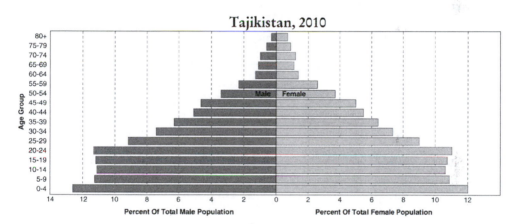

Figure 24 Tajikistan, 2010 (population pyramid)

Much of the labor force is in agriculture, raising cotton, wheat, fruits and vegetables. Russia, China, Kazakhstan, Turkey and Uzbekistan are major trading partners. There is potential for hydroelectric development. The massive Roghun Dam is being constructed on the Vakhsh River which will generate considerable amounts of power. However, that could negatively impact the flow of the Amu Darya going to Uzbekistan.

Uzbekistan

The Republic of Uzbekistan is a doubly landlocked country of Central Asia and is the most populous country of the region. The word Uzbek could mean "independent" or be the name of a leader (Bey or Bek).

In Uzbek Ўзбекистон Республикаси (O'zbekiston Respublikasi)

Environment. Uzbekistan borders all of the Central Asian states: Kazakhstan, Kyrgyzstan, Tajikistan, Turkmenistan as well as Afghanistan. The country's environment varies from the Fergana Valley in the east to the Kyzyl Kum (Red Desert) in the west. The Amu Darya used to flow to the Aral Sea, but the southern portion of the lake has shrunk severely. Much of the western portion of the country is desert. The Fergana Valley is better watered.

History. Bukhara and Samarkhand were settled very early by Indo-European and Persians in the sixth century BCE. The Greeks in the fourth century BCE, Arabs in the eighth century CE and Turks in the ninth century CE ruled in the area over a Persian population. Following the Mongols, Emir Timur ruled over the area from India to Baghdad in 1370–1405, establishing Samarkhand as a center, building monumental mosques, palaces and schools. Chagatai became a literary language along with Persian. By 1500 the Uzbek tribes from the north conquered the area and gave it its current name. Uzbeks had struggles with Persia, Kazakhs and Mongols. By the nineteenth century, Russia had moved southward to the Uzbek Khanates in Tashkent, Bukhara and Samarkhand. The country was a part of the Soviet Union from 1917 to 1991.

Population. Uzbekistan has a population of nearly 28 million, growing at 0.9 percent annually. Only 35 percent of the population are urban dwellers. Tashkent, the capital, with 2.2 million inhabitants, is the largest city in Uzbekistan and in Central Asia. Samarkhand is the second largest city at 390,000. Uzbeks are 80 percent of the population with a minority of Russian, Tajik, Kazakh and Karakalpak. Many Uzbeks in the south have a Tajik culture that comes under the government's official designation of Uzbek. There are many Uzbeks in Afghanistan and Tajikistan.

Culture. The Uzbek language is Turkic with many Persian, Arabic and now Russian words. After independence in 1991 the state began a shift from Cyrillic to Latin script, but that has not been completed. Most Uzbeks are Sunni Muslim. The Tajik minority speaks an Iranian language; Kazakh and Karakalpak are related languages. All are Muslim. Russian is a common language and there are many Orthodox churches, but not many Protestant churches. Examples of Uzbek cuisine include *plov* (rice pilaf), *shorpa* (soup), *kebabs* and tea. There is a rich literary, music, film and theater tradition in Tashkent and other urban centers.

Geopolitics. While Uzbekistan is a republic, power resides solely with Islam Karimov, who has been the chief leader since 1990. Uzbekistan has experienced border tensions with Kyrgyzstan and Tajikistan. Uzbekistan joined the Shanghai Cooperation Organization and the USA used Uzbek airbases to start the war on the Taliban in Afghanistan. Relations with the USA were good until 2005, when the Andizhan massacre in Fergana Valley came to light. Karimov takes his cue from Emir Timur as he tries to build Uzbekistan into the center of Central Asia.

Development. Uzbekistan has a per capita GDP of $3,000. Much of the labor force is in rural areas in agricultural jobs. Cotton is the main crop, with the country being the second largest cotton exporter. Wheat, rice, fruits and vegetables are other crops grown. Over-irrigation and over-use of chemicals have spelled a disaster for both the Amu Darya and the Aral Sea. The major export earners include natural gas, oil and gold. There is still a strong literacy rate, but the large youth population will require more education and jobs for continued development.

Turkmenistan

Turkmenistan borders Iran, Afghanistan, Uzbekistan and Kazakhstan. The country is well known for its natural gas, and, in the past, a very eccentric leader. "Turkmen" means "pure Turk," with "men" acting as an intensifer.

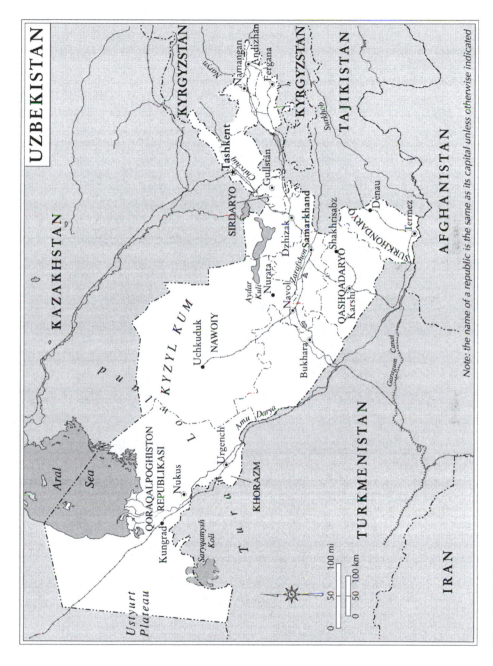

Map 65 Uzbekistan

Table 10 Uzbekistan – country facts

Land area	447,400 km^2
Population	28.13 million
Capital	Tashkent 2,201,000
Population density (persons per km^2)	62
Predominant religions	Muslim 88% (mostly Sunni)
Life expectancy at birth	72.0 yrs.
Under 5 mortality rate (per 1,000)	43
Access to improved water source (%)	87
GNI per capita	$2,910
Area as cropland (%)	0.8
Leading agriculture	Cotton; vegetables; fruits; grain; livestock
Leading industry	Food-processing; machinery; textiles; gold; petroleum; nat. gas
Merchandise trade (% of GDP)	56.1
Foreign direct investment (% of GDP)	1.0
Internet users (%)	4.5
Carbon dioxide emissions per capita (metric tons)	5.3

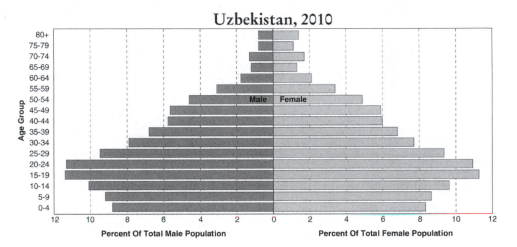

Figure 25 Uzbekistan, 2010 (population pyramid)

In Turkmen *Türkmenistan.*

Environment. The Garagum (Black Desert) covers much of the land. The Kopet-Dag Range marks the border with Iran. The Amu Darya in the north provides water to the large Garagum Canal. The canal waters the south all the way to the capital, Ashgabat. The climate is quite dry. The Caspian Sea provides linkages to Russia, Kazakhstan, Azerbaijan and Iran. Like Uzbekistan, over-irrigation and reliance on cotton production has severely depleted the soil. Petroleum products have also fouled the Caspian Sea.

History. Indo-European tribes such as Scythians (Saka) settled in the area by 2000 BCE. As in other areas in Central Asia, Greeks, Persians and Arabs controlled the territory. The

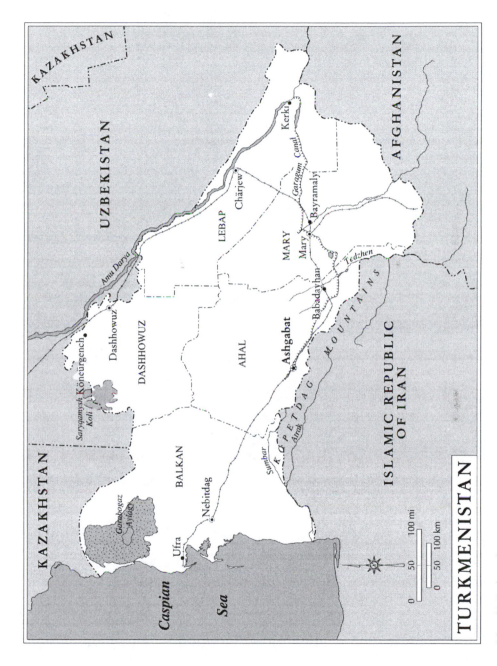

Map 66 Turkmenistan

Table 11 Turkmenistan – country facts

Land area	488,100 km²
Population	5.0 million
Capital	Ashgabat 637,000
Population density (persons per km²)	10
Predominant religions	Muslim 89%; Eastern Orthodox 9%
Life expectancy at birth	68.0 yrs.
Under 5 mortality rate (per 1,000)	51
Access to improved water source (%)	83
GNI per capita	$6,980
Area as cropland (%)	0.14
Leading agriculture	Cotton; grain; livestock
Leading industry	Natural gas; oil; petroleum products
Merchandise trade (% of GDP)	103.5
Foreign direct investment (% of GDP)	7.0
Internet users (%)	1.4
Carbon dioxide emissions per capita (metric tons)	8.7

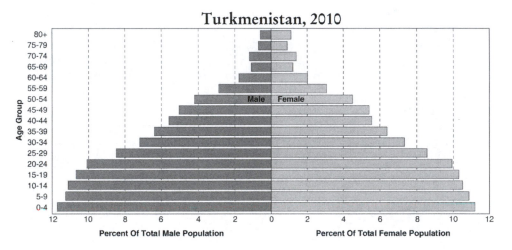

Figure 26 Turkmenistan, 2010 (population pyramid)

advent of Turkic Oghuz tribes in the eighth century CE preceded the Seljuk in the eleventh century. The Turkmen were part of these Oghuz tribes. The Mongols in the thirteenth century and Timur in the fourteenth ruled the Turkmen. From 1400 to the 1700s, Turkmen formed tribal confederations. Through the nineteenth century Russian forces moved into the area, and thousands of Turkmen were killed near Ashgabat in 1881. Resistance to Bolshevik rule was strong. The Turkmen Soviet Socialist Republic was a part of the Soviet Union from 1921 to 1991.

Population. Turkmenistan has 5 million people with a population growth rate of 1.1 percent. Half of the population are urban dwellers. Ashgabat, the capital, has 700,000 inhabitants, Chärjew (Turkmenabat) has 250,000, Dashhowuz (Daşoguz) has 200,000 and

Mary (Merv) has 100,000. Turkmen account for 85 percent of the population, with Russians and Uzbeks the main minorities.

Culture. Turkmen is a Turkic language and is shifting from a Cyrillic to a Latin script. Turkmen traditional culture is nomadic. Carpet motifs identify tribes and are found in the state flag and state emblem. Moderate Islam is followed in Turkmenistan. There are many Turkmen in Iran and Afghanistan. The Turkmen are related to the Salar in Qinghai.

Geopolitics. Saparumat Niyazov, who styled himself Tukmenbashy, the head of the Turkmen, ruled from 1985 to 2005. He built a gold statue of himself, renamed months after individuals in Turkmen history including family members, and banned the circus for not being Turkmen. His successor, Gurbanguly Berdimuhamedow, has moderated the policies. Still the former Communist Party, which is now the Democratic Party, is the only party in the country. Human rights are routinely abrogated. Turkmenistan became an associate member of the CIS in 2005 to maintain neutrality.

Development. Turkmenistan has a per capita GDP of $7,500 mostly due to its natural gas and oil exports. Half of the population still works in agriculture, producing cotton for export and wheat. Unemployment and poverty rates are high. New pipelines in 2010 to China and to Iran have added to outlets for gas and oil. The major trading partners include Ukraine, Turkey, Russia and China.

Caspian Sea

The Caspian Sea bridges Central Asia and the Caucasus subregions. The Caspian is the largest enclosed body of water on earth and is more properly identified as a lake as there is no connection to the oceans. Kazakhstan, Turkmenistan, Iran, Azerbaijan and Russia bound the lake.

Physical geography. Several major rivers flow into the Caspian, including the Volga from Russia, the Ural and Zhem from Kazakhstan, the Kura from Azerbaijan, and the Qezel Owzan from Iran. The Amu Darya at one time flowed into the Caspian, then to the Aral Sea, but does not now reach either. As there is no outflow, the Caspian is slightly saline. The Volga provides most of the water for the Caspian. The northern portion of the sea is relatively shallow and freezes over in winter, while the southern portion is quite deep.

Name. The name Caspian Sea refers to the Persian *Caspi*, an ancient people living near the sea in modern-day Iran/Azerbaijan. In Turkic languages the sea is called the Hazar denizi which means the Khazar Sea. The Khazars were a Turkic group that had a nomadic empire north of the Caspian.

Economy and envrionment. There are two main products of the Caspian. Caviar comes from the eggs of the sturgeon and oil comes from the wells (see Map 36 Caspian Sea Oil and Gas). Pollution from the oil wells is a problem in Kazakhstan and Azerbaijan, and overfishing of the sturgeon is also a problem. Since caviar is made from its eggs, the reproductive capacity of the sturgeon is threatened. The Volga has many factories on its banks. Pollution from the factories discharges into the Volga and thence to the Caspian.

Geopolitics. Iran has control over the southern end of the sea, while Turkmenistan and Azerbaijan divide the middle, and Russia and Kazakhstan divide the northern sector. Prior to the breakup of the Soviet Union, there were only two parties: the USSR and Iran. The main geopolitical issues are access to (1) oil and minerals, (2) fishing and (3) international waters. Map 36 shows the disposition of the oil deposits and indicates that Iran does not have much of the area's oil. The Volga–Don Canal provides access to the Black Sea. The

Map 67 Caspian Sea

political geography question is whether the Caspian is a lake or a sea. If the Caspian is a sea, then international law would mandate that all countries would have access. If the Caspian is a lake, then Russia does not have to grant access. So far the Caspian Sea countries are still in negotiation, having limited access to the sea themselves.

Caucasus

The Caucasus Mountains divide the Russian Federation from Georgia on the Black Sea coast, Azerbaijan on the Caspian Sea coast and land-locked Armenia. This area is also known as Transcaucasia.

Azerbaijan

The Republic of Azerbaijan is the largest of the countries in the Caucasus and borders Russia, Georgia, Armenia, Iran and Turkey. Azerbaijan refers to a Persian leader whose name meant the "land of the fire."

In Azeri Azərbaycan Respublikası.

Environment. The eastern area lies along the Caspian Sea, the northern area is in the Caucasus Mountains, and the center is in the Kura Lowland. Short rivers drain into the Caspian. The southeast is subtropical and dry. Baku is dry and mild. The major pollution sources include the oil fields along the Caspian which affect oil, air and water.

History. Indo-European people such as the Scythians settled here around 1000 BCE. Medes, Greeks, Seleucids and Albanians ruled here through 200 CE, followed by Persian Sassanids, Byzantines and Arab Abbasids till 1000. Oghuz and Seljuk tribes brought Turkic culture to the area. Caucasian and Iranian tribes converted to Islam and began to use the *Turkic languages*. After the Safavids in 1300–1600, local Turkic khanates ruled. By 1813, the Russians had arrived and fought with Iran over the khanates. With 1917 and the breakup of the Russian Empire, Azerbaijan, Georgia and Armenia joined as a republic. In 1918, the Azerbaijan Democratic Republic became independent. The Bolsheviks invaded in 1920 as the Soviet Union needed the oil of Baku. The Azerbaijan Soviet Socialist Republic was formed in 1920 and lasted till 1991.

Population. Azerbaijan has a population of 8 million with a growth rate of 0.8 percent. The level of urbanization is 52 percent. Baku is the primate city with a population of 1.9 million. Gäncä and Sumqayit have populations around 300,000. The population is 90 percent Azeri with smaller numbers of Dagestanis, Russians and Armenians. Armenians are located in Nagorno-Karabakh. There are another 12–19 million Azeris in Iran, as well as 800,000 in Turkey, 600,00 in Russia and 50,000 in Georgia.

Culture. Azeri is a Turkic language and has been written in a Latin alphabet since 1991. Many inhabitants also speak Russian. Azerbaijan is a secular state. A majority of the population is Shi'a Muslim. Dagestani is a Caucasus group which includes speakers of Lezgin and Avar. National traditions of Azeri culture are preserved in art, literature, dance and cuisine. Caspian fish, mutton, herbs, greens, saffron rice and black tea are typical components of a meal.

Geopolitics. Azerbaijan is a republic with many political parties. From 1991 to 1994 Azerbaijan was at war with Armenia over Nagorno-Karabakh. As a result there are many displaced persons. Hostilities have ended, but Azerbaijan does not control Nagorno-Karabakh. The current leader, Ilham Aliyev, succeeded his father, Heydar Aliyev, in office. Naxçivan lies separated from the rest of Azerbaijan's territory.

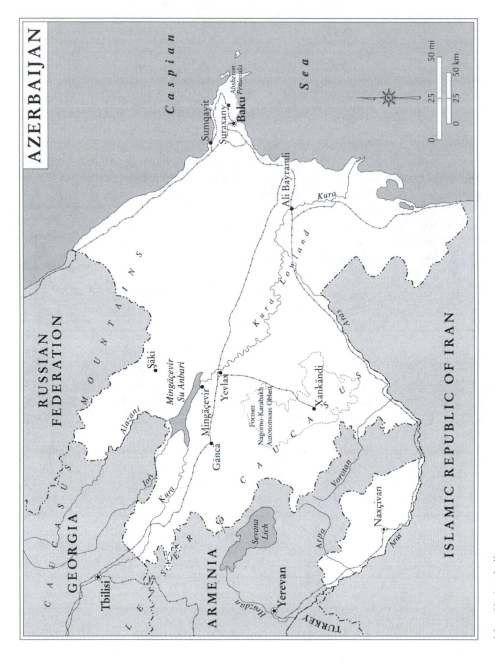

Map 68 Azerbaijan

Table 12 Azerbaijan – country facts

Land area	87,000 km²
Population	8.32 million
Capital	Baku 1,917,000
Population density (persons per km²)	102 per sq. mi.
Predominant religions	Muslim 93.4%; Russian Orthodox 2.5%
Life expectancy at birth	67.0 yrs.
Under 5 mortality rate (per 1,000)	88
Access to improved water source (%)	78
GNI per capita	$9,020
Area as cropland (%)	2.68
Leading agriculture	grain; cotton; grapes
Leading industry	petroleum; natural gas; steel; iron ore
Merchandise trade (% of GDP)	49.1
Foreign direct investment (% of GDP)	–2.8
Internet users (%)	12.3
Carbon dioxide emissions per capita (metric tons)	3.8

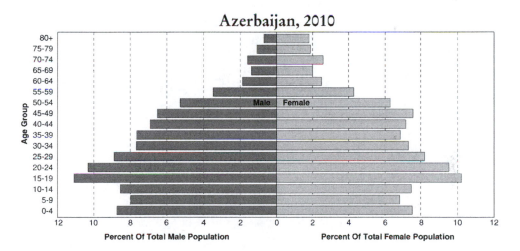

Figure 27 Azerbaijan, 2010 (population pyramid)

Development. Oil is the key resource. The GDP per capita is $10,000. Unemployment and poverty rates are low. Crops include cotton, grain, rice, fruits and vegetables. Oil and gas account for 90 percent of the exports with major customers being Italy, the USA, France, Israel and Russia. The Baku–Tbilisi–Ceyhan pipeline runs through Georgia to Turkey. The over-reliance on oil for exports is a continuing issue.

Armenia

The Republic of Armenia is a landlocked country and borders Georgia, Azerbaijan, Turkey and Iran. Armenians originally called their country Hayk' after their patriarch.

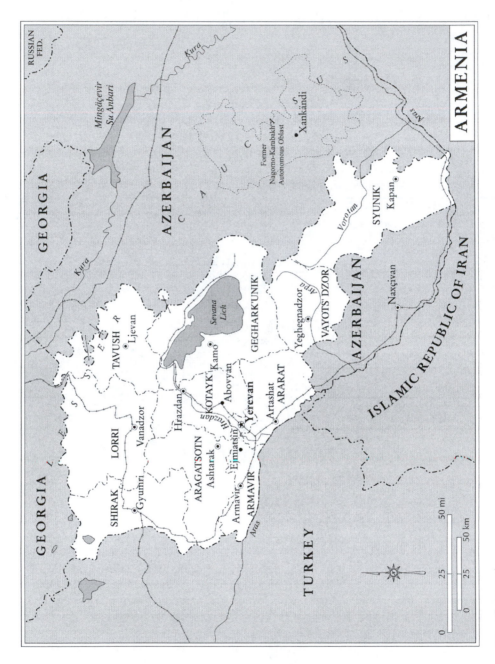

Map 69 Armenia

Table 13 Armenia – country facts

Land area	30,000 km²
Population	3 million
Capital	Yerevan 1,107,800
Population density (persons per km²)	107
Predominant religions	Armenian Apostolic 94.7%; Christian 4%
Life expectancy at birth	73.0 yrs.
Under 5 mortality rate (per 1,000)	24
Access to improved water source (%)	98
GNI per capita	$5,410
Area as cropland (%)	2.13
Leading agriculture	Fruits (grapes); vegetables; livestock
Leading industry	Machinery; chemicals; food-processing
Merchandise trade (% of GDP)	49.0
Foreign direct investment (% of GDP)	5.4
Internet users (%)	12.1
Carbon dioxide emissions per capita (metric tons)	1.2

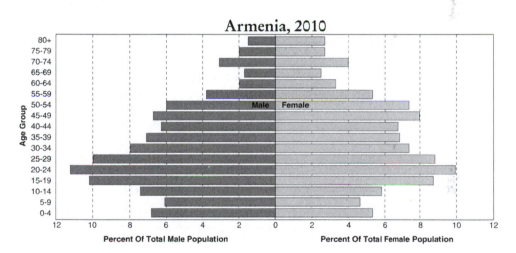

Figure 28 Armenia, 2010 (population pyramid)

In Armenian Հայաստանի Հանրապետություն (Hayastani Hanrapetut'yun).

Environment. Armenia is the smallest of the Caucasus states. The terrain is mountainous, mostly between 400 m (1,317 ft) and 4,000 m (13,120 ft) above sea level. The Lesser Caucasus forms the northern border with Georgia. The area is tectonically active. An earthquake heavily damaged the area in 1988. The Aras River flows into Azerbaijan. Lake Sevan (Sevana Lich) lies at 2,000 m (6,056 ft). Pollution is a worrisome issue, with some thinking it better to have industrial production with pollution rather than no production at all.

History. Yerevan, the modern capital, traces its history back to 782 BCE. The Armenian kingdom began in 600 BCE. Armenian kingdoms contended with the Sassanids, the Byzantines and the Seljuk Turks through 1000 CE. The Mongols and Timurids ruled from

1200 to 1500 BCE and the Ottomans and Persians divided the territory in the sixteenth century. Many Armenians lived in the Ottoman Empire. Russia ruled eastern Armenia in the 1800s. In World War I, the Ottomans killed as many as 1 million Armenians in a genocide between 1915 and 1917. After the Russian Revolution, Armenia joined Georgia and Azerbaijan in a republic in 1918. This was followed by Armenian independence from 1918 to 1922, when the Soviet Union annexed the country. From 1922 to 1936, it formed a Transcaucasus Socialist Federative Socialist Republic with Georgia and Azerbaijan. From 1936 to 1990, it was the Armenian Soviet Socialist Republic.

Population. Armenia has a population of 3 million with a 0.06 percent growth rate. The urbanization level is 64 percent. Yerevan, the capital, is the largest city at 1.1 million inhabitants, Gyumri has 160,000 and Vanadzor has 100,000. The population is 98 percent Armenian, with small percentages of Kurds and Russians. There is a great Armenian diaspora numbering 1 million in Russia, 500,000 in Iran, 500,000 in the USA, 400,000 in France and 300,000 in Georgia.

Culture. Armenian is an Indo-European language, with a script invented in 400 CE. Russian is a de facto second language. Armenia is the oldest Christian state, beginning in 300 CE. The Armenian Apostolic Church, separate from the Eastern Orthodox, dates back to 450 CE and accounts for 95 percent of the population. Cultural traditions in art, dance and music are maintained. Traditional foods include *lavash* bread and cracked bulghur wheat.

Geopolitics. The republic has free elections and several political parties. Continuing issues include the Armenian genocide, which has made relations with Turkey very difficult, and the war with Azerbaijan over Nagorno-Karabakh. Relations with Turkey are improving more than those with Azerbaijan. Nagorno-Karabakh operates as a de facto independent entity. Armenia has good relations with Iran and Russia to counterbalance Turkey and Azerbaijan.

Development. Armenia has a per capita GDP of $5,700 with a growth rate of 2.6 percent. Armenia depends a fair amount on Russian investment in infrastructure and management. The main exports include iron and copper. Major crops include fruits and vegetables, which are exported to Russia. Major trade partners are Germany, Russia, the USA and China. Economic difficulties are relieved by international remittance from its diaspora and international aid.

Georgia

Georgia has borders with Russia, Azerbaijan, Armenia and Turkey and a coastline on the Black Sea which allows it access to international waters. Its people call themselves Kartvelians and their name for the country, Sakartvelo, means a place for the Kartvelians. They are called Georgians because of their respect for Saint George.

In Georgian საქართველო (Sakartvelo).

Environment. The Great Caucasus Mountains form the border with Russia with peaks rising to 5,000 m (16,400 ft). The Lesser Caucasus Mountains lie in the south. Western and eastern Georgia have a humid subtropical climate, while Tbilisi has a humid continental climate.

History. Georgians had a kingdom beginning in 300 BCE, before the Romans conquered the area in 60 BCE. The Persians, Arabs and Turks also controlled the area later. Georgian kingdoms ruled from 800 to 1200 CE. The Mongols conquered in the thirteenth century and then Timur in the fourteenth. By the sixteenth century, the Persian and Ottoman empires split the territory, and in the nineteenth Georgia was absorbed into the Russian

Map 70 Georgia

Table 14 Georgia – country facts

Land area	70,000 km²
Population	4.59 million
Capital	Tbilisi 1,110,000
Population density (persons per km²)	64 per sq. mi.
Predominant religions	Orthodox Christian 83.9%; Muslim 9.9%
Life expectancy at birth	77.0 yrs.
Under 5 mortality rate (per 1,000)	32
Access to improved water source (%)	99
GNI per capita	$4,700
Area as cropland (%)	3.8
Leading agriculture	citrus; tea; wine
Leading industry	machinery; chemicals; scrap metal
Merchandise trade (% of GDP)	63.5
Foreign direct investment (% of GDP)	13.7
Internet users (%)	8.2
Carbon dioxide emissions per capita (metric tons)	0.9

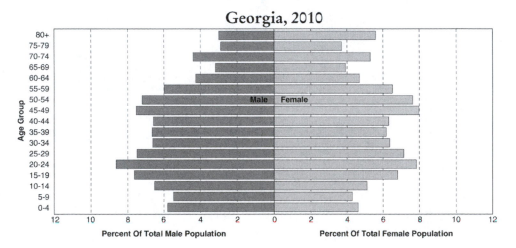

Figure 29 Georgia, 2010 (population pyramid)

Empire. After 1917, it was independent from 1918 to 1920. In 1921, Georgia was forced into the USSR, at first as part of the Transcaucasus with Armenia and Azerbaijan and then from 1936 to 1991 as the Georgian Soviet Socialist Republic.

Population. Georgia has a population of 4–5 million with a growth rate of –0.3 percent. The level of urbanization is 53 percent. Tbilisi, the capital, is the largest city with a population of 1.1 million. Kut'aisi has a population of 200,000. The population is 84 percent Georgian with Azeri and Armenian minorities. There are 200,000 Georgians in the European Union, 200,000 in Russia and 200,000 in the USA.

Culture. Georgian is a Caucasus language not related to any Indo-European languages and the alphabet in its modern form dates back to the fifth century CE. Georgia adopted Christianity by 319 CE. More than 80 percent of the population follow the Georgian Orthodox

Church. Azeri are Muslim and Armenians are also Christian. Georgian cuisine includes wine, dumplings and cheese bread.

Geopolitics. Georgia is a republic. Civil conflict marked 1991–92 and brought Eduard Shevardnadze to power. In 2003 the Rose Revolution deposed Shevardnaze and Mikheil Saakashvili was elected in 2004. In 2008 Georgia and Russia went to war over the breakaway republics of Abkhazia and South Ossetia. These two territories have declared independence and are recognized by Russia and several other countries. Georgia maintains good relations with the EU, NATO and the USA.

Development. Georgia has a per capita GDP of $4,900, which is growing at a rate of 6.4 percent. Major crops include citrus, grapes and tea. Major exports include metal, wine, mineral water, ores, fruits and vegetables. The country's major trade partners include Turkey, Azerbaijan, Armenia, Canada and Ukraine. Georgia gets oil from Azerbaijan via the Baku–Tbilisi–Ceyhan oil pipeline. Such transit corridors are useful in the Georgian economy.

10 Eurasian scenarios

In summary, we present briefly ten scenarios for Central Eurasia's future. We think it is important for scholars, specialists and practitioners to consider future demographic, economic, social and geopolitical events and developments that may shape this region in the coming decades. Scenarios are brief descriptions of likely events. They are based on our reading and understanding of current economic, demographic and political situations and events, and then a look into the possible scenarios for 2025, 2050 and beyond. Some of our scenarios will be more likely than others, for example, anticipated population changes, environmental conditions, social well-being measures and economic futures. Others, for example, looking at geopolitical worlds and political maps, may be less likely, and even controversial, but we realize that changes take place even in political arenas that affect political cultures, identities, alliances and boundaries. The ten scenarios are not listed in any priority.

1 Greater transboundary linkages and new economic unions. We envision greater cross-boundary economic, cultural and political cooperation in three locations: the Caucasus, Central Asia and western China. These will result in stronger economic ties among the current states in these three regions.

2 Preparing for a post-petroleum world. For states that currently have their economies linked to fossil fuels, especially oil and gas, they will need to plan for economies once the supplies of their non-renewable resources are reduced and exhausted. This is especially true for Azerbaijan, Kazakhstan, Turkmenistan and Uzbekistan. Future economic planning might focus on harnessing and exporting solar energy, tourism development, and greenhouse and sustainable agriculture.

3 Continued rise of secular Islamic states. In contrast to strict and fundamentalist Islamic states to the south of Central Eurasia, we envision most governments continuing their secular programs, which will include greater women's rights, the open tolerance of different religions and teaching of religious multiculturalism in the schools.

4 Diminished influence of Russia. Russia's influence will likely wane in the coming decades and be replaced by the rising influence of China. This region, aside from the Caucasus, is distant from Moscow and where most Russians live and where the central government is strong. While Russians will continue to live in each state, their proportion of the total populations will decline every decade and be replaced by growing numbers of people of indigenous Central Asian cultures. Russia also is likely to give this region a lower priority as it strengthens its economic and political ties with Europe.

5 The continuing rise of China. This scenario is already being played out in the marketplaces of Central Asia and west China. The greater amount of goods produced in China and the growing influence of Chinese merchants and funding development projects are ample evidence that China will continue to strengthen its economic and political ties, especially in Central Asia.

6 *Environmental disasters waiting to happen.* This region has acute environmental disasters that are not being solved or improving. These include the drying up of the Aral Sea, which will eventually be a huge salt flat with pesticides and insecticides on the surface that will contribute to declining health standards among those living nearby. Another is the drawing down of the Caspian Sea and the use of very marginal agricultural lands, for example, in the Kazakhstan steppes, for grain production. Another is likely to be the effects of global warming, which might bring to the region higher temperatures, desertification, receding glaciers, and the drying up of tributaries currently used for productive agriculture. These and other environmental disasters are attributed to human decisions, that is, the reduction of waters entering the Aral Sea, pollution of the Caspian, cultivation of marginal lands and cutting down forests on hillsides.

7 *Kazakhstan as the regional leader.* Kazakhstan, because of its size, wealth, central location and borders with six countries, will be the key player in the region's economic and political future. How it spends its dollars, its aid programs to neighboring states, and its role as the key negotiator in troubled spots merit close attention. The country should be a key player in promoting greater rights for women, cleaning up the environment, welcoming competing groups into the political process and being the negotiator between China and Russia with their prospective testy relations. According to the Population Reference Bureau, a standard source used for population projections, Kazakhstan is expected to increase its population from 16 million in 2010 to 21 million in 2050; Uzbekistan, the largest country in Central Asia, will likely see its population grow from 28 million to 42 million. Tajikistan will grow by about 5 million, Kyrgyzstan about 2.6 million and Turkmenistan 1.6 million.

8 *Flashpoints on the political map.* As previous maps have illustrated, the Central Eurasian region is not immune to both low-level conflicts and longer wars (Tajikistan). It is unlikely these will subside in the future; rather they are expected to remain and possibly increase. The flashpoints, some of which may be cross-border in nature, may intensify not only in the Caucasus region, but also in western China, especially Xinjiang and Tibet, as well as Central Asia. Kyrgyzstan, Uzbekistan and Tajikistan are countries with strong subnational regional sentiments, which are often against the central government. Kazakhstan has thus far not faced major conflicts, but potentially it could in southern, northern and western regions.

9 *Cultural changes.* The world's cultural map is changing with globalization, increased transportation and communication contacts with nearby and distant places, and greater internationalization in the marketplaces, entertainment and religious spheres of life. The social and political impacts of the Internet revolution and all it entails are difficult to predict, but if the events of 2011 are any indicator, there will likely be some unintended consequences to youth and marginal groups wishing to be empowered by these new technologies and demanding greater voices in political, economic and cultural spheres.

10 *Redrawing the political map.* We can envision several scenarios, all of which would result in a redrawing of the Central Eurasian political map. These could include the following: (a) a breakup of existing political units with the result being a number of new states and enlarged existing states; (b) an enlarged and stronger China and the merging of existing Central Asian and Caucasus states into a new CIS; (c) a series of microstates or city states; (d) a Central Eurasian Union (much like the European Union); (e) a new enlarged state called Turkestan; or (f) a similar entity called Altaistan.

Behind these shifts in boundaries would be on-the-ground changes in regards to independent and collective aspirations of majority and minority ethnic groups, possibly a stronger

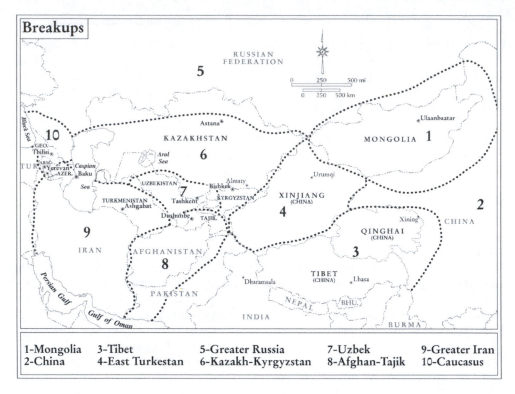

Map 71 Breakups

1-Mongolia 3-Tibet   5-Greater Russia   7-Uzbek   9-Greater Iran
2-China   4-East Turkestan 6-Kazakh-Kyrgyzstan 8-Afghan-Tajik 10-Caucasus

Map 72 CIS/PRC Split

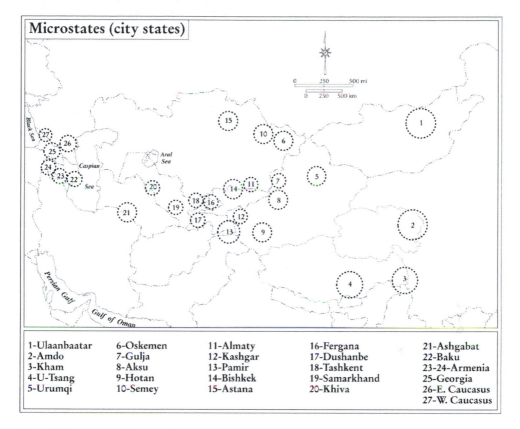

Microstates (city states)

1-Ulaanbaatar	6-Oskemen	11-Almaty	16-Fergana	21-Ashgabat
2-Amdo	7-Gulja	12-Kashgar	17-Dushanbe	22-Baku
3-Kham	8-Aksu	13-Pamir	18-Tashkent	23-24-Armenia
4-U-Tsang	9-Hotan	14-Bishkek	19-Samarkhand	25-Georgia
5-Urumqi	10-Semey	15-Astana	20-Khiva	26-E. Caucasus
				27-W. Caucasus

Map 73 Microstates (city states)

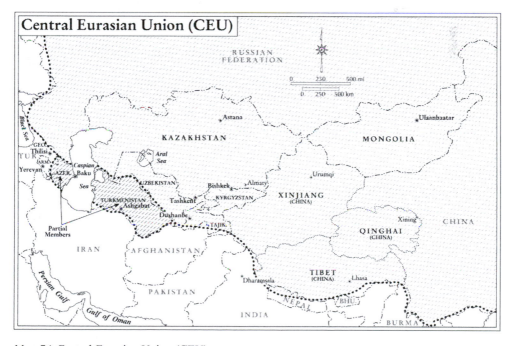

Map 74 Central Eurasian Union (CEU)

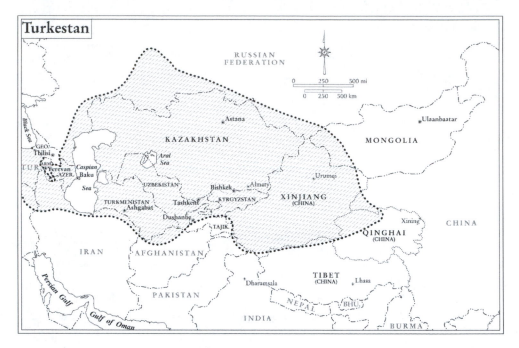

Map 75 Turkestan

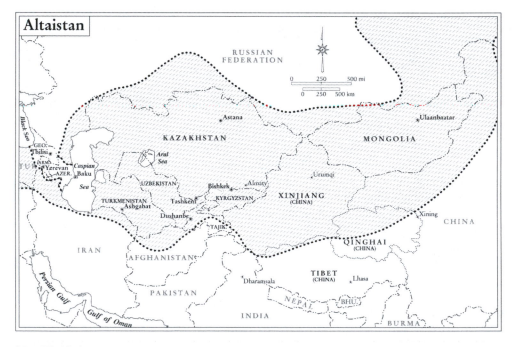

Map 76 Altaistan

and far-reaching influence of China in the region, an enlarged CIS with Russia playing the key role, and new confederations such as Turkestan and Altaistan. There might also be a series of breakups and mergers. Mergers might result in a CIS that would include all of the Caucasus and Central Asian states, and an enlarged China that would include Mongolia and also parts of eastern Kazakhstan and Kyrgyzstan. Breakups might include China without historical Tibet, East Turkestan and Greater Mongolia (Inner and Outer). Mergers might include northern Kazakhstan joining Russia, Tajikistan merging with Afghanistan, Azerbaijan into Iran, Armenia and Georgia merging, and Uzbekistan including all of the Fergana Valley and southern Kyrgyzstan. A series of micro (city) states might also appear, including Samarkhand, Bukhara, Tashkent, Fergana-Osh, Kashgar, Urumqi, Turkmen, Mongol, Almaty, Astana, Semey, Ust-Kamenogorsk (Oskemen) and others. There might also be a CEU (Central Eurasian Union) as one state that would include China, Russia, Kazakhstan, Kyrgyzstan, Tajikistan, Uzbekistan, Turkmenistan and Mongolia. This state would be based on the Shanghai Cooperative Organization.

These six maps are speculative and meant for discussion; whether any will actually depict the political map in 2050 or 2075 is not the major issue. Our reason for including these is to keep in mind that the map of this region has changed in the past twenty, fifty and one hundred years. There is little reason to think the "final political map has been drawn."

One certainty for the region is that Greater Eurasia, and Central Asia in particular, will continue to be a key region in European and Asian geopolitics and geoeconomics, simply because of its location. The countries and leaders will seek to carve out a unique role for this region in continental and global affairs, a region that is not European, not East Asian and not South Asian, but one that is Central Eurasian.

Table 15 Imperial/USA to metric (SI) conversion table and vice versa

IMPERIAL/USA TO METRIC (SI) CONVERSION TABLE

Symbol	When you know	Multiply by length	To find	Symbol
in	inches	25.4	millimeters	mm
ft	feet	0.305	meters	m
yd	yards	0.914	meters	m
mi	miles	1.61	kilometers	km
		Area		
in^2	square inches	645.2	square millimeters	mm^2
ft^2	square feet	0.093	square meters	m^2
yd^2	square yards	0.836	square meters	m^2
ac	acres	0.405	hectares	ha
mi^2	square miles	2.59	square kilometers	km^2
		Temperature		
°F	Fahrenheit	$(F{-}32) \times 5/9$ or $(F{-}32) / 1.8$	Celsius	°C

continued

Table 15 continued

METRIC (SI) TO IMPERIAL/USA CONVERSION TABLE

Symbol	When you know	Multiply by length	To find	Symbol
mm	millimeters	0.039	inches	in
m	meters	3.28	feet	ft
m	meters	1.09	yards	yd
km	kilometers	0.621	miles	mi

		Area		
mm^2	square millimeters	0.0016	square inches	in^2
m^2	square meters	10.764	square feet	ft^2
m^2	square meters	1.195	square yards	yd^2
ha	hectares	2.47	acres	ac
km^2	square kilometers	0.386	square miles	mi^2

		Temperature		
°C	Celsius	1.8C + 32	Fahrenheit	°F

Bibliography

Atlases

Abazov, Rafis. 2008. *The Palgrave Concise Historical Atlas of Central Asia*. New York: Palgrave Macmillan.

Allen, John L. 2010. *Student Atlas of World Geography*. Boston: McGraw-Hill.

Asian Development Bank. 2012. *Central Asia Atlas of Natural Resources*. Manila, Philippines: Asian Development Bank.

Barnes, Ian, Robert Hudson and Bhikhu C. Parekh. 1998. *The History Atlas of Asia*. Macmillan Continental History Atlases. New York: Macmillan.

Bater, James H. 1989. *The Soviet Scene: A Geographical Perspective*. New York: Routledge.

Bater, James H. 1996. *Russia and the Post-Soviet Scheme*. New York: Wiley.

Benewick, Robert, and Stephanie Donald. 2009. *The State of China Atlas: Mapping the World's Fastest-Growing Economy*. Berkeley: University of California Press.

Boyd, Andrew, and Joshua Comentz. 2007. *An Atlas of World Affairs*. New York: Routledge.

Brawer, Moshe. 1994. *Atlas of Russia and the Independent Republics*. New York: Simon & Schuster.

Bregel, Yuri. 2000. *Historical Maps of Central Asia 9th–19th Centuries AD*. Papers on Inner Asia Supplement. Bloomington; Indiana University, Research Institute for Inner Asian Studies.

Bregel, Yuri. 2003. *An Historical Atlas of Central Asia*. Leiden and Boston: Brill.

Channon, John. 1995. *The Penguin Historical Atlas of Russia*. London and New York: Penguin.

Chinese Academy of Sciences, Institute of Geography. 2000. *The Atlas of Population, Environment and Sustainable Development of China*. Beijing and New York: Science Press.

Cooke, Tim. 2010. *The New Cultural Atlas of China*. Tarrytown, NY: Marshall Cavendish.

Gilbert, Martin. 2007. *The Routledge Atlas of Russian History*. London and New York: Routledge.

Hedin, Sven. 1966. *Central Asia Atlas*. Stockholm: Statens Etnografiska Museum.

Herb, Guntram H. 2006. *Perthes World Atlas*. Goths, Germany: Klett.

Herrmann, Albert, Norton Sydney Ginsburg, Paul Wheatley and Albert Herrmann. 1966. *An Historical Atlas of China*. Chicago: Aldine.

Hewsen, Robert H., and Christopher C. Salvatico. 2001. *Armenia: A Historical Atlas*. Chicago: University of Chicago Press.

Jacobson-Tepfer, Esther, James E. Meacham and Gary Tepfer. 2010. *Archaeology and Landscape in the Mongolian Altai: An Atlas*. Redlands, CA: ESRI Press.

Kennedy, Hugh, Marc Bel and Peter van der Donck. 2002. *An Historical Atlas of Islam/Atlas historique de l'Islam*. Leiden: Brill.

Milner-Gulland, R. 1998. *Cultural Atlas of Russia and the Former Soviet Union*. New York: Checkmark Books.

National Geographic. 2008. *Atlas of China*. Washington, DC: National Geographic Society.

Robinson, Francis. 1982. *Atlas of the Islamic World since 1500*. New York: Facts on File.

Ruthven, Malise, and Azim Nanji. 2004. *Historical Atlas of the Islamic World*. Derby, UK: Cartographica.

Schwartzberg, Joseph E., and Shiva G. Bajpai. 1992. *A Historical Atlas of South Asia*. New York: Oxford University Press.

Shinjang Uighur Aptonom Rayonluq Ölchăsh-Sizish Idarisi and Xinjiang Weiwu'er Zizhiqu min zu yu wen gong zuo wei yuan hui. 2005. *Shinjang Uighur Aptonom Rayoni khăritilăr toplimi* (*Xinjiang Uyghur Autonomous Region Atlas*). Beijing: Junggo Khărită Năshriyati.

Shuler, Martin *et al*. 2004. *Gornyĭ atlas Kyrgyzstana* (*Mountain Atlas of Kyrgyzstan*). Bishkek: NSC; Lausanne: EPF.

TSegmid, Sh and Vladimir Voro'bev. 1990. *Bugd Nairamdakh Mongol Ard Uls, Undesnii Atlas* (*National Atlas of the Mongolian People's Republic*). Ulaanbaatar.

United Nations. 1998. *Geology and Mineral Resources of Kyrgyzstan*. New York: United Nations.

United Nations. 1999. *Geology and Mineral Resources of Mongolia*. New York: United Nations.

United Nations. 2000. *Atlas of Mineral Resources of the ESCAP Region. Vol. XV: Geology and Mineral Resources of Azerbaijan*. New York: United Nations, Economic and Social Commission for Asia and the Pacific.

Uzbekistan khalq talimi vazirligi. 1999. *Ŭzbekiston geografik atlasi* (*Uzbekistan Geographical Atlas*). Tashkent: DIK Nashriëti.

Vardanyan, Mamluk. 2009. *Atlas Nagorno-Karabakhskoĭ Respubliki* (*Atlas of Nagorno-Karabakh Republic*). Erevan: GNO "TSentr geodezii I kartografii.".

World Bank. 2009. *Atlas of Global Development*. Washington, DC: World Bank.

Zhurinov, M. Zh. 2011. *Bol'shoĭ Atlas Kazakhstana* (*Great Atlas of Kazakhstan*). Moscow: Dizaĭn, Informatsiia, Kartografiia.

Books

Ascher, William, and N. S. Mirovitskaiia. 2000. *The Caspian Sea: A Quest for Environmental Security*. Dordrecht: Kluwer Academic.

Beckwith, Christopher I. 2009. *Empires of the Silk Road: A History of Central Eurasia from the Bronze Age to the Present*. Princeton: Princeton University Press.

Blinnikov, Mikhail. 2011. *A Geography of Russia and its Neighbors*. New York: Guilford.

Boulnois, Luce. 2004. *Silk Road: Monks, Warriors and Merchants on the Silk Road*. New York: Norton.

Bradshaw, Michael, George W. White, Joseph P. Dymond, and Elizabeth Chacko. 2011. *Essentials of World Regional Geography*. Boston: McGraw-Hill.

Brunn, Stanley D., Maureen Hays-Mitchell and Donald J. Zeigler (eds.). 2012. *Cities of the World: World Regional Urban Development*. 5th edition. Lanham, MD: Rowman and Littlefield.

Cannon, Terry (ed.). 2000. *China's Economic Growth: The Impact on Regions, Migration and the Environment*. London: Macmillan.

Chinn, Jeff, and Robert Kaiser. 1996. *Russians as the New Majority: Ethnicity and Nationalism in the Soviet Successor States*. Boulder, CO: Westview Press.

Clawson, David L., and Merrill L. Johnson. 2004. *World Regional Geography*. Upper Saddle River, NJ: Pearson, Prentice Hall.

Davis, Elizabeth V. W. and Rouben Azizian. 2007. *Islam, Oil, and Geopolitics: Central Asia after September 11*. Lanham, MD: Rowman & Littlefield.

De Young, Alan. 2010. *Lost in Transition: Redefining Students and Universities in Contemporary Kyrgyz Republic*. Charlotte, NC: Information Age Publishing.

Diener, Alexander C. 2004. *Homeland Conceptions and Ethnic Integration among Kazakhstan's Germans and Koreans*. Lewiston, NY: Edwin Mellon Press.

Gamer, Robert (ed.). 2011. *Understanding Contemporary China*, Boulder, CO: Lynne Rienner.

Gaubatz, Piper R. 1996. *Beyond the Great Wall: Urban Form and Transformation on the Chinese Frontiers*. Stanford, CA: Stanford University Press.

Gleason, Gregory. 2003. *Markets and Politics in Central Asia: Structural Reform and Political Change*. London and New York: Routledge.

Goldstein, M. 1997. *The Snow Lion and the Dragon*. Berkeley: University of California Press.

Hanks, Reuel R. 2005. *Central Asia: A Global Studies Handbook*. Santa Barbara, CA: ABC-CLIO.

Hobbs, Joseph J. 2007. *Fundamentals of World Regional Geography*. Belmont, CA: Brooks-Cole.

Lattimore, Owen. 1940. *Inner Asian Frontiers of China*. New York: American Geographical Society.

Lattimore, Owen. 1950. *Pivot of Asia: Sinkiang and the Inner Asian Frontiers of China and Russia*. Boston: Little, Brown.

Levi, Scott Cameron, and Ron Sela. 2010. *Islamic Central Asia: An Anthology of Historical Sources*. Bloomington: Indiana University Press.

Lewis, Robert A. (ed.). 1992. *Geographic Perspectives on Soviet Central Asia*. New York: Routledge.

Polo, Marco. *The Travels*. Harmondsworth: Penguin, various editions.

Pope, Hugh. 2006. *Sons of the Conquerors: Rise of the Turkic World*. New York: Overlook Press.

Pryde, Philip R. 1995. *Environmental Resources and Constraints in the Former Soviet Republics*. Boulder, CO: Westview Press.

Pulsipher, Lydia M., and Alex Pulsipher. 2006. *World Regional Geography: Global Patterns, Local Lives*. New York: W. H. Freeman.

Rowntree, Les, Martin Lewis, Marie Price and William Wyckoff. 2006. *Diversity amid Globalization: World Regions, Environment, Development*. Upper Saddle River, NJ: Pearson, Prentice Hall.

Seymour, James D., and Richard Anderson. 1998. *New Ghosts, Old Ghosts: Prisons and Labor Reform Camps in China*. Armonk, NY: M. E. Sharpe.

Shaw, Denis J. B. 2006. *Russia in the Modern World: A New Geography*. Malden, MA: Blackwell.

Starr, S. Frederick. 2004. *Xinjiang: China's Muslim Borderland*. Armonk, NY: M. E. Sharpe.

Veeck, Gregory, Clifton W. Pannell, Christopher J. Smith and Youqin Huang 2011. *China's Geography: Globalization and the Dynamics of Political, Economic, and Social Change*. Lanham, MD: Rowman & Littlefield.

Journal articles and book chapters

Anacker, Shonin. 2007. Geographies of Power in Nazerbayev's Astana. *Eurasian Geography and Economics*, Vol. 45, No. 4, pp. 515–33.

Bassins, David, Ben DeRudder, Peter J. Taylor, Pengfei Ni, Michael Hoyler, Jim Huang and Frank Witlox. 2010. World City Network Integration in the Eurasian Realm. *Eurasian Geography and Economics*, Vol. 51, No. 3, pp. 385–410.

Batbayar, Tsedendamba. 2002. Geopolitics and Mongolia's Search for Post-Soviet Identity. *Eurasian Geography and Economics*, Vol. 43, No. 4, pp. 323–35.

Becker, Charles M., Erbolat N. Musabek, Ai-Gul S. Seitenova and Dina S. Urzhumova. 2003. Short-Term Migration Responses of Women and Men during Economic Turmoil: Lessons from Kazakhstan. *Eurasian Geography and Economics*, Vol. 44, No. 3, pp. 228–43.

Blinnikov, Mikhail, and Megan E. Dixon. 2011. Mega-engineering Projects in Russia: Examples from Moscow and St. Petersburg. In: S. D. Brunn (ed.), *Engineering Earth: The Impacts of Megaengineering Projects*. Dordrecht, The Netherlands: Springer, pp. 933–54.

Bond, Andrew R. and Natalie R. Koch. 2010. Interethnic Tensions in Kyrgyzstan: A Political Geographic Perspective. *Eurasian Geography and Economics*, Vol. 51, No. 4, pp. 531–62.

Brunn, Stanley D. 2003. A Note on Hyperlinks of Major Eurasian Cities. *Eurasian Geography and Economics*, Vol. 44, No. 4, pp. 321–24.

Brunn, Stanley D. 2011. Fifty Years of Nuclear Testing in Semipalatinsk, Kazakhstan: Juxtaposed Worlds of Blasts and Silences, Security and Risks, Denials and Memory. In: S. D. Brunn (ed.), *Engineering Earth: The Impacts of Megaengineering Projects*. Dordrecht, The Netherlands: Springer, pp. 1789–920.

Brunn, Stanley D., Jeffrey Jones and Darren Purcell. 1994. Ethnic Communities in the Evolving "Electronic State." In: Werner Gallusser (ed.), *Political Boundaries and Co-Existence*. Berne and New York: Peter Lang, pp. 415–29.

Cathcart, Richard and Viorel Badescu. 2011. Aral Sea Partial Refilling Project. In: S. D. Brunn (ed.), *Engineering Earth: The Impacts of Megaengineering Projects*. Dordrecht, The Netherlands: Springer, pp. 1541–48.

Cohen, Saul B. 2005. The Eurasian Convergence Zone: Gateway or Shatterbelt? *Eurasian Geography and Economics*, Vol. 46, No. 4, pp. 1–22.

Demirbag, Mehmet, Ekrem Tatoglu and Adiya Oyungerel. 2005. Patterns of Foreign Direct Investment in Mongolia, 1990–2003. *Eurasian Geography and Economics*, Vol. 46, No. 4, pp. 396–18.

Diener, Alexander C. 2011. Will New Mobilities Beget New (Im)Mobilities? Prospects for Change Resulting from Mongolia's Trans-State Highway. In: S. D. Brunn (ed.), *Engineering Earth: The Impacts of Megaengineering Projects*. Dordrecht, The Netherlands: Springer, pp. 627–42.

Engelmann, Kurt. 1998. Central Asia and "Levels" of Development. *Education about Asia*, Spring, pp. 36–42.

Foster, Benjamin D. 2011. Empire, Names and Renaming: The Case of Nagorno Karabach. In: S. D. Brunn (ed.), *Engineering Earth: The Impacts of Megaengineering Projects*. Dordrecht, The Netherlands: Springer, pp. 2013–30.

Frank, Andre Gunder. 1992. The Centrality of Central Asia. *Bulletin of Concerned Asian Scholars*, Vol. 24, pp. 50–74.

Gentile, M. 2003. Delayed Underurbanization and the Closed-City Effect: The Case of Ust-Kamenogorsk. *Eurasian Geography and Economics*, Vol. 2, pp. 144–56.

Goodman, David S. G. 2004. The Campaign to "Open Up the West": National, Provincial-level and Local Perspectives. *China Quarterly*, Vol. 178, pp. 317–34.

Gosar, Anton. 2011. Energy-Hungry Europe: Development Projects in South-Central Europe. In: S. D. Brunn (ed.), *Engineering Earth: The Impacts of Megaengineering Projects*. Dordrecht, The Netherlands: Springer, pp. 447–60.

Hanks, Reuel R. 2000. Emerging Spatial Patterns of the Demographics, Labour Force and FDI in Uzbekistan. *Central Asian Survey*, Vol. 19, No. 3/4, pp. 351–66.

Harris, S. A. 2011. The Qinghai–Tibetan Railroad; Innovative Construction on Warm Permafrost in a Low-Latitude, High-Elevation Region. In: S. D. Brunn (ed.), *Engineering Earth: The Impacts of Megaengineering Projects*. Dordrecht, The Netherlands: Springer, pp. 747–65.

Holzlehner, Tobias. 2011. Engineering Socialism: A History of Village Relocation in Chukotka, Russia. In: S. D. Brunn (ed.), *Engineering Earth: The Impacts of Megaengineering Projects*. Dordrecht, The Netherlands: Springer, pp. 1957–74.

Iwasaki, Ihiro. 2002. Observations on Economic Reform in Tajikistan: Legislatiave and International Framework. *Eurasian Geography and Economics*, Vol. 43, No. 6, pp. 493–504.

Kaminski, Bartlomiej, and Gaël Raballand. 2009. Entrepôt for Chinese Consumer Goods in Central Asia: The Puzzle of Re-exports through Kyrgyz Bazaars. *Eurasian Geography and Economics*, Vol. 50, No. 5, pp. 327–47.

Kuchukeeva, Altinay, and John O'Loughlin. 2003. Civic Engagement and Democratic Consolidation in Kyrgyzstan. *Eurasian Geography and Economics*, Vol. 44, No. 8, pp. 557–86.

Micklin, Philip. 2002. Water in the Aral Sea Basin of Central Asia: Cause of Conflict or Cooperation? *Eurasian Geography and Economics*, Vol. 43, No.7, pp. 505–28.

Micklin, Philip. 2006. The Aral Sea Crisis and its Future: An Assessment in 2006. *Eurasian Geography and Economics*, Vol. 47, No. 5, pp. 546–67.

Micklin, Philip. 2011. The Siberian Water Transfer Scheme. In: S. D. Brunn (ed.), *Engineering Earth: The Impacts of Megaengineering Projects*. Dordrecht, The Netherlands: Springer, pp. 1515–30.

Myant, Martin, and Jan Drahokoupil. 2008. International Integration and the Structure of Exports in Central Asia. *Eurasian Geography and Economics*, Vol. 48, No. 5, pp. 604–22.

Nekrich, A. 2011. Character and Scale of Environmental Disturbances Resulting from Mining in the Kursk Magnetic Anomaly. In: S. D. Brunn (ed.), *Engineering Earth: The Impacts of Megaengineering Projects*. Dordrecht, The Netherlands: Springer, pp. 413–28.

O'Hara, Sarah, and Michael Gentile. 2009. Household Incomes in Central Asia: The Case of Post-Soviet Kazakhstan. *Eurasian Geography and Economics*, Vol. 50, No. 3, pp. 327–47.

O'Hara, Sarah, Artjoms Ivlevs and Michael Gentile. 2009. The Impact of Global Financial Crisis on Remittances in the Commonwealth of Independent States. *Eurasian Geography and Economics*, Vol. 50, No. 4, pp. 447–63.

O'Lear, Shannon. 2004. Resources and Conflict in the Caspian Sea. *Geopolitics*, Vol. 9, No. 1, pp. 161–66.

O'Lear, Shannon. 2007. Azerbaijan's Resource Wealth: Political Legitimacy and Public Opinion. *Geographical Journal*, Vol. 173, No. 1, pp. 207–23.

O'Loughlin, John, Vladimir Kolossov and Jean Radvanyi. 2007. The Caucasus in a Time of Conflict: Demographic Transition and Ordinary Russians. *Eurasian Geography and Economics*, Vol. 48, No. 2, pp. 135–56.

Pannell, Clifton W. 2007. The China Challenge: Observations on the Outlook for the 21st Century. *Eurasian Geography and Economics*, Vol. 48, No. 1, pp. 3–15

Pannell, Clifton W. 2011. China Gazes West: Xinjiang's Growing Rendezvous with Central Asia. *Eurasian Geography and Economics*, Vol. 52, No. 1, pp. 105–18.

Rowe, William C. 2011. Turning the Soviet Union into Iowa: The Virgin Lands Scheme in the Soviet Union. In: S. D. Brunn (ed.), *Engineering Earth: The Impacts of Megaengineering Projects*. Dordrecht, The Netherlands: Springer, pp. 237–56.

Toops, Stanley. 2003. Xinjiang (Eastern Turkistan): Names, Regions, Landscapes, Futures. In Chiao-min Hsieh (ed.), *Changing China*. Boulder, CO: Westview Press, pp. 411–21.

Toops, S. 2004. *Demographics and Development in Xinjiang after 1949*. Washington, DC: East West Center. Working Papers, No. 1.

Warf, Barney. 2009. The Rapidly Evolving Geographies of the Eurasian Internet. *Eurasian Geography and Economics*, Vol. 50, No. 5, pp. 564–80.

Werner, C. 2003. The New Silk Road: Mediators and Tourism Development in Central Asia. *Ethnology*, Vol. 42, No. 2, pp. 141–59.

Werner, Cynthia, and Kathleen Purvis-Roberts. 2006. After the Cold War: International Politics, Domestic Policy and the Nuclear Legacy in Kazakhstan. *Central Asian Survey*, Vol. 25, No. 4, pp. 461–80.

Werner, Cynthia, and Kathleen Purvis-Roberts. 2007. Unraveling the Secrets of the Past: Contested Versions of Nuclear Testing in the Soviet Republic of Kazakhstan. In: B. Johnson (ed.), *Half-lives and Half-truths: Confronting the Radioactive Legacy of the Cold War*. Santa Fe: School for Advanced Research Press, pp. 277–98.

Yacher, Leon. 2011. Astana, Kazakhstan: Megadream, Megacity, and Megadestiny? In: S. D. Brunn (ed.), *Engineering Earth: The Impacts of Megaengineering Projects*. Dordrecht, The Netherlands: Springer, pp. 1001–20.

Yeh, Emily T. 2009. From Wasteland to Wetland? Nature and Nation in China's Tibet. *Environmental History*, Vol. 14, No.1, pp. 103–37.

Websites

Armenia Government http://www.gov.am/en/
Azerbaijan Government http://www.azerbaijan.az/portal/index_e.html
Blacksmith Institute of Most Polluted Sites http://www.blacksmithinstitute.org
Cambridge Central Asia Forum http://www.cambridge-centralasia.org/
The Central Asia – Caucasus Institute Analyst http://www.cacianalyst.org/
China Internet Information Center http://www.china.org.cn/english/index.htm
China Dimensions http://sedac.ciesin.org/china/
Central Eurasian Studies Society http://centraleurasian.org/
Central Tibetan Administration http://tibet.net/
China's Prisons http://en.wikipedia.org/wiki/File:Laogai_Map.jpgfile
Electronic Cultural Atlas Initiative Silk Road Atlas http://ecai.org/silkroad/
EurasiaNet http://www.eurasianet.org/

Ferghana Information Agency http://enews.fergana.com/
HH Dalai Lama http://www.dalailama.com/
Kazakhstan Government site http://en.government.kz/
Kyrgyz embassy to US http://www.kgembassy.org/
Miami Silk Road Project http://www.orgs.muohio.edu/silkroad/index.html
Mongolia Government http://www.pmis.gov.mn/pmis_eng/index.php
Nuclear Threat Initiative http://nti.org/e_reserach/gmap/
People's Republic of China http://www.gov.cn/english/
President of Georgia http://www.president.gov.ge/
Radio Free Asia http://rfa.org/english/
Radio Free Europe Radio Liberty http://www.rferl.org/
Tibetan Exile Administration http://www.tibet.com
Silk Road Foundation http://www.silk-road.com
Silk Road Project http://www.silkroadproject.org/
Silk Road Seattle http://depts.washington.edu/uwch/silkroad/index.shtml
Tajikistan US Embassy http://www.tjus.org/
Turkmenistan embassy to US http://www.turkmenistanembassy.org/
United Nations Human Development Report, 2007/2008 http://hdr.undp.org/en/media/HDR_20072008_
    EN_iondicar_tables.pdf
United Nations Gender Inequality Index http://hdrstats.undp.org/en/indictors/68606.html
Uzbekistan Government http://www.gov.uz/en/
Uzbekistan US Embassy http://www.uzbekistan.org/

Index of places

Please note that page references in *italics* indicate maps, graphs or tables.

Index of proper names and terms

Please note that page references in *italics* indicate maps, graphs or tables.

Index of topics, themes and concepts

Please note that page references in *italics* indicate maps, graphs or tables.

Printed and bound by PG in the USA

USA2010PGIL